Praise for *The Membership Organization*

"The self-motivation of employees that occurs in the membership organization may be the only truly sustainable competitive advantage. This book targets right in on that crucial, and too often overlooked, ingredient for success."

> Carter T. Funk
> Vice President
> Consolidated Natural Gas

"An outstanding contribution to the business/management literature. This book will be highly valued not only for corporate executives and organization development consultants, but also to city managers, and civil society organization executives in the field of improving the performance of their fellow workers and stakeholders."

> Dr. Akhtar Badshah
> Executive Director
> Asia-Pacific Cities Forum

"In *The Membership Organization,* Jane Seiling offers an innovative and provocative approach to organizational behavior. She provides a practical understanding of how to create and manage a workplace which invites membership, high performance, and productivity from everyone in the organization. This is a must read book for managers and consultants wanting to understand the workforce of the new millenium."

> Diana Whitney
> Whitney & Associates
> Taos, NM

"Jane's message is that if we begin to truly value the member, the member will value customers and the products and services they produce. My recommendation is for all members to read this book, use the knowledge and the logic, and apply it rightly. That is how true ownership by all members will be achieved."

> Robert K. Huff
> Robert K. Huff & Associates
> Consultant to management and unions

The Membership Organization

The
Membership
Organization

Achieving Top Performance Through the New Workplace Community

Jane Galloway Seiling

Foreword by David Noer

DAVIES-BLACK PUBLISHING
Palo Alto, California

Published by Davies-Black Publishing, an imprint of Consulting Psychologists Press, Inc., 3803 East Bayshore Road, Palo Alto, CA 94303; 1-800-624-1765.

Special discounts on bulk quantities of Davies-Black books are available to corporations, professional associations, and other organizations. For details, contact the Director of Book Sales at Davies-Black Publishing, an imprint of Consulting Psychologists Press, Inc., 3803 East Bayshore Road, Palo Alto, CA 94303; 650-691-9123; Fax 650-988-0673.

The section on philanthropy in Chapter 4 was written in collaboration with James Gregory Lord, Philanthropic Quest International, Cleveland, Ohio.

Cover illustration: © Jose Ortega/SIS

01 00 99 98   10 9 8 7 6 5 4 3 2
Printed in the United States of America

Library of Congress Cataloging-in-Publication Data
Seiling, Jane G.
     The membership organization : achieving top performance through the
  new workplace community / Jane Galloway Seiling; foreword by David Noer.
       p. cm.
     Includes bibliographical references and index.
     ISBN 0-89106-110-X
     1. Decision-making, Group.   2. Management—Employee participation.
3. Community.   4. Organizational change.   I. Title
    HD30.23.S44   1997
    658.4'036—dc21   97-26478
                                                                CIP

FIRST EDITION
First printing 1997

*This book is written, with love,
for Maggie, Sam, and Tucker Jones,
my wonderful grandchildren,
in hopes that someday they will work
in Membership Organizations.*

Contents

Foreword

As we watch the last grains of sand trickle from the hourglass of the old millennium, we are also experiencing the last days of another familiar institution: the bureaucratic orientation of our organizations. This is at once compelling and distressing: despite the rallying cries of managers, consultants, and politicians to "stomp out bureaucracy" and make our organizations more responsive and fluid, we are deeply, though often unconsciously, conditioned to connect with our organizations from a bureaucratic frame of reference.

Classic bureaucracy has been given a bad rap. As originally articulated by German sociologist Max Weber at the turn of the century, the concept made organizations more rational and tied promotions and pay to merit rather than to birthright (Kasler, 1988). It gave us job descriptions, merit pay, role-based performance appraisal, formal succession planning, and the overall philosophical perspective of separation of the office from the officer. However, the dark side of classic bureaucracy—the fixed, rigid inflexibility—is anathema to the new-millennium organization. The problem is that we don't know how to replace Weberian bureaucracy. Many of our deeply held values concerning motivation, loyalty, and commitment have their roots in it. Our notions of long-term employment and equating pay increases and perquisites to promotion and loyalty to organization rather than profession are rooted in classic bureaucratic assumptions that are very difficult to drop. As a frustrated general manager, struggling to help his organization move away from dysfunctional bureaucratic assumptions, expressed it, "Bureaucracy is dead, but we don't know how to bury it!"

In his book *The Structure of Scientific Revolutions,* Thomas Kuhn (1980) chronicled many of the fundamental shifts in worldview, which he called *new paradigms,* that took place in the last millennium. The concept of a round world and not a flat one was a full-blown paradigm shift. The shift from Newton's fixed and unchangeable universe to one of relativity and chaos is another. For those of us who spend our lives in organizations, the shift from a fixed, long-term, bureaucratic connection with our organizations to one that is more fluid and flexible is just as profound. In order to let go of the old, no-longer-functional bureaucratic connection with our organizations, we need a new vision, something to hold on to. Organizational leaders of the new millennium need the same faith and vision as did Christopher Columbus when he operationalized his paradigm shift to the unproved but dogmatic belief that he wouldn't sail off the edge of the earth. The same general manager who was looking for a bureaucratic graveyard went on to tell his co-workers that they had to make a basic change or, as he said it, "We've got to work on our own little paradigm shift!" He understated the problem for effect, and I know he would agree that it is a very profound shift in worldview that new-millennium leaders must confront.

In order to operate with some degree of sanity and control in the confusion and ambiguity of the new-millennium organization, we need a frame of reference—a way to discover a degree of coherence. Toward this end, Jane Seiling has written a very important book that offers both an anchor and a vision. The language of membership provides a needed focus and grounding. We gain both a collective purpose and individual ownership. The principles of membership give us a sense of direction and grounding in the postbureaucratic void we all experience. Above all, the prospect of Membership Organizations provides hope and optimism for both organizational productivity and the relevance and humanity of those of us who spend our working lives in organizational systems.

David Noer
Greensboro, North Carolina
April 1997

Acknowledgments

Putting my beliefs and experiences on paper was a labor of love. It is amazing to me that my family and friends survived it all. For this reason, I want to acknowledge my husband, Bill Seiling, for his patience during all the years when "experience" was collected; my children, Terri Jones, Michael Caputo, and Stacy Seiling, for listening when the subject would not go away; my twin, Janet McCormick, who served as first editor, challenger, and cook; my mother, Irene Galloway, for her sustaining grace; and my late father, Sam Galloway, the first leader I ever knew.

My thanks also for the "talking-to's," contributions, and unflagging support of Kenneth Gergen, Sue Hammond, Penny Groscost, Tina Searcy, and Amy Mullen.

I would also like to acknowledge those who, over the years—some without their awareness—contributed to the formulation of this model. The list of their names is too long to be included here, but that in no way diminishes the significance of their contributions. Some of the contributions were very positive, and some were more difficult "learning events" that were nonetheless important. Of course, though the journey has been long, it will never end.

I would also like to thank Melinda Adams Merino of Davies-Black Publishing for her support and encouragement. Without her belief this book would not have happened. Her patience and fortitude were exemplary, and her enthusiasm cannot be matched. My debt to her is not repayable.

Finally, it is appropriate that I acknowledge the five CEOs and COOs I worked for during the early years of my career as a secretary and assistant. It was during this time that I formed many of the thoughts and beliefs reflected in the following pages of this book. As is always true, most of those learning events were positive, some were not so positive. Nonetheless, these leaders helped me see the potential for everyone in the organization to contribute to its welfare. My appreciation goes to:

- The first leader, who taught me that I could do more than I ever dreamed and that what I did mattered
- The second leader, who taught me that not standing up for what you believe turns control over to others—silence is not golden
- The third leader, who taught me that our actions "tell" people what each of us believes in
- The fourth leader, who taught me that strong, healthy leadership can happen only when we connect to the people we are leading, that relationships and accountability matter, wherever you are in the organization
- The fifth leader, who taught me that fear is not motivating and that one can learn even in the worst of circumstances

1

Our concept of organizations is moving away from the mechanistic creations that flourished in the age of bureaucracy. We have begun to speak in earnest of more fluid, organic structures, even of boundaryless organizations. We are beginning to recognize organizations as systems, construing them as "learning organizations" and crediting them with some type of self-renewing capacity.

Margaret J. Wheatley,
Leadership and the New Science

The Membership Principles

It is not surprising that leaders want to create a new way of working. The old way, with the "inner circle" controlling, no longer works. The inner circle must be expanded to include all members of the workplace community in the responsibility of actively contributing to achievement. In an article in the *Harvard Business Review,* Mintzberg (1996) suggests that the organization is a circle, with the leaders in the center. Around the edges are the people who know the everyday operations of the organization. Although their view is limited to their own perspective, their ability to contribute to the welfare of the overall organization is no longer questioned. Within the expanded circle, the boundaries that separate the leaders from the other members are blurred, making it easier for all to work together.

Working together must indeed become easier. Leaders now know that the effective organization must create an inclusive, more accepting environment, where everyone has respect and dignity. Leaders have decided it is time to open opportunities to deeper participation and involvement by all so that real innovation is possible. But how can this be done? It is increasingly obvious that it is essential to get top performance from people in all areas of the circle. A new workplace scenario reflecting a new mind-set—a community of connected people who care more deeply about their organization—is needed.

The Old Mind-Set

The old way of working offered token gestures inviting participation while withholding true permission to take action. This is counterproductive and keeps the inner circle intact and remote. Employees sense that competence and influence are related to their ability to be top performers. When they achieve competence in their jobs, they want to exert influence. When this opportunity does not materialize, the feeling of competence decreases—and a self-fulfilling prophecy begins: When they feel competent, they want to be influential; otherwise, they feel incompetent. Frustration, cynicism, and disconnection follow. They may refuse to provide input even when asked, wearing like a badge a negative impression of the workplace community. This badge is inevitably noticed, even accepted as valid, whether the observer be boss, co-worker, customer, family member, or friend.

Consider the impact of withholding, withdrawal, separation, and limited participation on the bottom lines of organizations. New products are designed every day without input from those who will make, sell, and buy them. Because members are allowed no opportunity to give practical input, customers are kept out of the process and end up buying—or refusing to buy—something that does not meet their needs. Redesigning or adapting the product, or eventually pulling it from the market or liquidating at a loss because it did not sell, is costly. This adds to the original investment in a product that *could* have been designed to meet customer needs in the first place.

Limiting employee involvement can also directly affect feelings of community, raising barriers to group interactions in the organization. Supervisors who discount the knowledge and input of subordinates eventually dry up a resource for innovative and creative change in work processes. Secretaries whose input is not valued lower their antennae regarding what is happening in the areas they work in, and the leaders they report to lose active opportunities to address issues from the perspective of one who frequently interacts on the front line. When signals are given that what the customer says is irrelevant, marketing persons stop carrying messages back to their group. When suggestions are ignored, workers stop making them. As a result, the organization can become increasingly dysfunctional in its ability to achieve organizational goals.

Each workplace community has its own "laws" regarding how things work. These laws may differ markedly from the personal guidelines an individual applies to his or her own work. A member who values the opportunity to talk things through may be signaled that "silence is golden" or "just tell me when you're done." Conversely, a member who thinks things through well on his or her own may be chastised for "not being a team player." Formal and informal rules, processes, and procedures control group activity. Such practices may be rigid, limiting, and even destructive to the individual's impetus toward peak performance. When an employee protests the controls that keep him or her from top performance, leaders try to bring the "irrational" protester into line. Nonconformists make managers nervous: What if they encourage others to voice their concerns? Could things get out of control?

The New Workplace Community

Community means connections among groups over time. The term evokes images of belonging and pride, a symbolic home. Transferring those images to a *workplace community*—a workplace that is moral and respectful, and that treats employees as *responsible agents* of the organization—is highly desirable.

People seek to work in a community where they feel connected to the success and purpose of the organization. In such an organization, employees *want* to be top performers, participating deeply in the success of a workplace community in which they share ownership of mission and purpose. Such a workplace community directly influences the comfort or discomfort of the individual member. The community collectively decides who is hired, based on standards established over

> ## The New Workplace Community
>
> **Is inclusive, integrative, and flexible** Recognizing that
> members of the community are diverse in background,
> skills, and needs makes it possible to see that differences
> can have a positive impact on the survivability of the orga-
> nization. Communities thrive when groups tap these
> resources, listen to and learn from alternative perspetives,
> and are open to the influence of members at all levels.
> Flexibility and adaptability are possible when innovation
> and creativity are encouraged and attention is given to
> visionary compatibilities of ideas, visions, and worldviews
> of all members.
> **Sets goals that attract the input of organizational members**
> Each member has the opportunity to offer information
> and input in setting goals and working toward organiza-
> tional success. The member feels pride in the accomplish-
> ments of the past and sees the organization's future as
> hopeful.
> **Encourages collaborative partnerships** Cross-community
> partnerships increase the sharing of expertise and make it
> possible to challenge the status quo. These partnerships
> expand available information and create opportunities
> to coordinate mechanisms that influence how members
> work together. Member interdependence and indepen-
> dence are seen as important to the achievement of mas-
> tery both individually and organizationally.
> **Communicates effectively** Providing and seeking informa-
> tion, answering questions, and keeping channels of dis-
> cussion open eliminate surprises and reinforce feelings of
> trust and belief in the organization..

time; who fits into the internal community; and how to behave
on the job (what to say and whom to say it to). These collective
decisions establish feelings of solidarity within the community,
based on signals of appropriateness given and reinforced by the
organizational leaders. Because members spend eight to ten (or
more) hours a day within the community, how they feel during
those hours can directly affect how they feel off the job as well.

Community suggests an organization that is beneficial, productive, and interconnected. People work well together because

> ## The New Workplace Community (continued)
>
> **Instills pride in organizational membership** Members want to feel proud of the organization they represent. Pride in connection to the organizational community is attributed to successful, balanced consideration, and achievement in all three bottom lines. The *human* bottom line requires the organization to consider decisions based on the impact on the organizational membership, both individually and collectively. The *social* bottom line requires the organization to be ethical in how work is done, the products or services it is providing, and its connection to the community it is serving. The *financial* bottom line requires the organization to make rational, logical, long-term focused decisions.
>
> **Is steadfast in difficult situations** When faced with difficult times, the organization considers long-term alternatives that make it possible to keep the membership stable. Members at all levels are willing to make sacrifices and to participate in identifying solutions that are beneficial to the long-term existence of the organizational community.
>
> **Understands that the phrase "we are the organization" is significant to the success of the workplace community** The organization recognizes that although it is a collective community, the individual member can affect the success of the company. For this reason, the success of the organization is tied to respect for the success of the individual *and* the community it represents.

they are interdependent *and* autonomous. Applying the concept of community to the workplace suggests new definitions of how both the individual and the organization achieve top performance.

An End to Excuses

In an interview, Peter Block stated, "Much of what we do is well-meaning cosmetics. In many cases we've just become *more articulate* about empowerment with no re-distribution of power and choice. And nothing fundamental has changed" (Block's italics) (p. 5). The term *cosmetics* connotes an effort to cover up what is actually happening, providing ample room for excuses and behind-the-scenes games that merely imply member participation. A new workplace community is needed in order for an organization to get to and move beyond participation to true empowerment and enrollment of its members. This community must include forums of involvement that allow for a boundaryless, co-constructed relationship. Members are limited only by their own choice of how much to contribute.

Telling ourselves that the limitations of the hierarchical, bureaucratic organization cannot be erased is succumbing to the undeniable evidence of lowered organizational performance or even threats to organizational survival. A whole world of pent-up energy, frustrated dedication, and underutilized problem-solving abilities can be released by eliminating the authoritarian, controlling ways traditionally in use. Failure to do so is to limit profits, foster cynicism, curtail innovation, and at best maintain the status quo.

The Environment of Emergence

The new workplace community encourages members to re-enroll and to assume ownership of and responsibility for the organization's performance and success. This will require a change in the way employees work together and new recognition of individual and organizational potential. Peter Block states, "Every aspect of organizing human effort needs reform. Mission statement, structure, work process, teamwork, the role of the boss, the pay system, information systems, measurements, controls—all the practices and underlying beliefs that we have grown up with, and with which we have succeeded, are now in question" (McLagan & Nel, 1996)

The words *every aspect* imply the need to go beyond the processes of leading through control to acceptance of higher member responsibility for personal behaviors, beliefs, working standards, and actions. Cynical organizations paint dismal pictures of organizations that are not "perfect." In order to create a brighter canvas of workplace communities, we must change ways of working. The cynical organization is not cynical by accident; cynicism is the result of lack of attention to the needs of the

CHART 1 Signs of Organizational Functioning	
Cynical	Emergent
Denies issues	Confronts issues appropriately
Does not listen	Listens and learns
Localizes knowing at the top of the pyramid	Pushes knowing, doing, and accountability across the organizational circle
Perpetuates mistrust	Offers and receives trust
Requires perfection	Encourages learning events
Fosters separation	Seeks cooperation
Is unforgiving	Supports, values, and forgives

employees, maintenance of concepts of "superiority" and "inferiority," and shared mistrust. Working in a cynical environment feels bad, creating frustrations that never seem to go away with all the accompanying signs of discontent. Although organizations are constantly in the process of organizing, certain signs indicate how the workplace membership experiences that process (see Chart 1).

In 1978, Jack Gibb discussed trends that he predicted would affect the future of organizing. One of those trends was the *environment of emergence:*

> *The emergent form will be a practical and attainable model of group and institutional life, supplanting the participative model.* The current model toward which practitioners, organizational-development consultants, theorists, and social engineers have been aiming is a "skilled-leader-with-active-participants" form. . . . The growing recognition that the participative model is but a transitional step . . . is creating a cultural readiness for new practical images of social life. . . . This breakthrough will make possible a new age of creativity, productivity, ecstasy, and fulfillment. (Gibb's italics; p. 282)

It is obvious that Gibb's "new age of creativity, productivity, ecstasy, and fulfillment" has been slow in coming. The workplace community is now ready for the next level of involvement. Employees are ready to work with instead of for the leaders of organizations, and to assume responsibility for the success or failure of their organizations. *The employees are ready for real membership in their workplace communities.*

The Language of Membership

Membership indicates a workplace environment where members choose to work in the organization—even if they feel they *must*, for economic reasons, work in the organization. In the Membership Organization, the members individually and collectively work beyond participation. There is a mind-set of high personal responsibility, shared accountability, and member connectedness, making it possible for a more level working community to exist. The concept of *membership* stimulates enrollment in the organizational purpose, facilitates acceptance of a shared urgency of top performance, and expands opportunities for contribution and success for every individual and group within the workplace community.

The Language of Membership

Looking at how new ways of working emerge into possibility and then actuality means creating new theory and deliberate language to discuss and shape into values the envisioned reality. These values are linked to the culture, systems, structures, and processes inside the community. Ford and Ford (1995, p. 542) state that in order for an intentional change to happen, "new realities are created, sustained, and modified in the process of communication. . . . [It] is a matter of deliberately bringing into existence . . . a new reality or set of social structures."

New language encourages the formation of new meanings. Of course, in order for a new language to mean anything others must understand it and find it appropriate. Otherwise it will make no sense (Weick, 1995). Once sense is made of the language within the workplace community, there is a possibility of it being absorbed into relationships. Thus there is potential for transformation (Gergen & Thatchenkery, 1996).

In an effort to make sense of the new realities in the workplace, the concept of *membership* is suggested as a way of thinking and working together in our organizations. As such, membership is a symbolic reference and a way of framing and describing the collective working group.

Membership by Choice

The language of membership intentionally indicates that the employees have made a conscious choice to become members of this particular organizational community—no one forced them to seek employment with XYZ Company. Nor do employees abdicate responsibility for their own welfare when they are hired. In the Membership Organization™, the dependency that was sustained by the hierarchical environment of the past is replaced with member awareness that high performance is important not only to personal success but also to the overall success of the workplace community. For this reason, membership stimulates the fullest development of all to the highest level of empowerment, involvement, partnership, and innovation. Employability, or the willingness to take action to remain a sustaining part of the organization, is the responsibility of employees even while their actions benefit the organization.

As part of a Membership Organization, leaders also acknowledge that employees make conscious or unconscious choices regarding their level of contribution and participation, and they understand that organizational climate and physical environment can make a difference in those choices. For this reason, it is important to maintain a positive workplace environment.

The Inclusivity of Membership

The term *member* in the Membership Organization is used as a replacement for *employee*. As such, the term *member* is all encompassing: Members reside at all levels of the organization; they include the CEO, secretaries, vice presidents, hourly members, managers, directors, professionals, supervisors, part-time members, contractors—everyone at every level and in every relationship within the workplace community. Although accountable for assigned activities, members assume a position based on the situation of the moment and their own accountabilities. A member may be a leader on this project and not on the next, blurring the lines of status and position. He or she will

defer to and seek out the knowledge and experience of appropriate others, whatever their stance in the organization, thereby
expanding the range of exchanged information.

It is significant to note that at all levels within the membership
organization *each individual's responsibility to contribute to and
participate in maximization of the bottom lines of the organization to the limits of his or her ability is not only accepted but
encouraged, and even expected.* The willingness of the member
to participate to the fullest is an extension of the organization's
desire and ability to create an accepting, forgiving, and inclusive
workplace community. The member's role is to individually
accept and project the responsibility and the discipline required
to nurture top performance in the membership environment.

Membership as a Mind-Set

The term *follower* is sometimes used in formulating a new social
contract that emphasizes the "courage to be right, the courage to
be wrong, the courage to be different from each other." The
leader and follower share a common purpose in order for the
organization to accomplish and succeed (Chaleff, 1996, p. 4).
Kelley (1992) states, "In reality, followership and leadership are
separate concepts, two separate roles. They are complementary,
not competitive, paths to organizational contribution" (p. 41).
Kelley also states that "followership and leadership are dialectic.
Just as the word *right* makes no sense without *left,* they depend
upon each other for existence and meaning" (p. 45).

However, *member* (a person who belongs to a group or organization) and *membership* (the state of being a member) incorporate the definitions of *follower* (an adherent, disciple) and
leader (guide, chief, director) without the connotation of separation and the strongly implied negative consequences of *supervisor* or *manager*—with the insinuation of localized power. (Power
is often seen as negative by followers deprived of it.)

A dichotomy exists in the use of the words *employee* and
member. The designation of *employee* as subordinate (1) reflects
the old divisive way of command and control; (2) indicates that
permission is required to step out of the box of status quo; (3)
limits employee actions and responses to "doing" in specific

CHART 2 Organizational Mind-Set	
Hierarchical	Membership
Participants divided into *managers* and *employees*	All participants considered members
Divisiveness	Inclusiveness
Permission needed	Deep participation
Employees limited to doing	Thinking and doing across the circle
Closed system	Open system
Management as experts	All members as experts
Status significant to functioning	Contribution across blurred lines

areas; (4) uses bureaucracy and hierarchical divisiveness to actively keep employees in their place; and (5) locates expertise, innovation, and "thinking" at higher levels in the organization. Chart 2 shows the contrasts.

In the Membership Organization: (1) members are recognized as competent in the roles they perform while at the same time encouraged to expand possibilities of performance; (2) actions of informal leadership are normal occurrences and recognized as vital to the success of the group and the organization; (3) member opportunities to be empowered are limited only to the extent of the member's willingness and ability; (4) the member is encouraged to question the status quo and is individually and collectively challenged to stretch and grow; and (5) individual member performance is seen as significant to the success and achievement of the group and the organization.

Membership as Meaning

The term *membership* indicates that members choose to work in the organization. This implies free choice—members voluntarily join and stay in the organization. The concept of freedom of choice eliminates the member's sense of helplessness and hopelessness and enhances the new psychological contract between the member and the organization. The victim mentality of the past disappears when membership by choice prevails.

Membership participants know that the new psychological contract does not include permanent employment, that there is no guarantee of lifetime employment in this particular job or even in this workplace community. Members understand that they are not "entitled" to the benefits, paycheck, or retirement plan that were included in the old contract, so they actively participate in maximizing their own employability and in doing so help perpetuate their employment and their organization. Even though the old contract is disintegrating before their eyes, they are reinforcing the existence of their organization and the possibility of its long-term survival. David Noer (1997) says that "when workers choose to stay in organizations because of the work and the customers, knowing they may not be able to stay for an entire career—they all tend to be much more productive and committed" (p. 8).

Upon hearing that the organization is experiencing lowered customer evaluation numbers, a member with a positive response to lack of security understands that personal income or employment may be at stake and knows that what is done individually matters to those numbers. This member accepts the choice of individually contributing to the improvement of those numbers through his or her own actions (increased personal responsibility). A person who discounts a personal ability to affect the numbers (lack of responsibility) perpetuates a negative feeling of insecurity by withholding increased participation in addressing customer issues (while probably pointing fingers and blaming others). A member who acknowledges that the new contract does not guarantee employment has the opportunity to ensure employment at a higher level by learning, innovating, and contributing at a higher level. Those who contribute positively to organizational survival will be the ones most able to guarantee their own employment security as well as the security of the overall organization. Thus, individual feelings of a lack of security motivate positive members to work beyond participation, becoming more productive and committed to workplace performance, while heightening the security of existence for the overall workplace community.

Both the members and the organization are learning not to be helpless and hopeless while watching the train approaching—

they are, as a workplace community, making a choice to build new tracks in a new direction.

Beyond Participation

The Membership Organization, with its mind-set of chosen responsibility, appropriate accountability, and member connectedness, allows for a more level working community. For this reason, the members individually and collectively choose to work beyond participation in transcommunity partnerships. Working beyond participation is a personal choice where deep involvement increases respect and dignity at all levels, escalating the overall contribution of the collective membership. Members ask strong questions, seek reasons, innovate spontaneously, and work beyond the expected—because they want to, not because they "should" do so. There is a desire for contribution that pulls the group toward a common need to participate in the sucess of the organization and each other.

Beyond participation reflects a state of high enrollment that strengthens the members' sense of ownership and urgency regarding overall personal and organizational performance. Working beyond participation is built on member knowledge and understanding of the (1) existence of the authority to act, (2) right to perform offered by the collective community and accepted by the individual member, (3) responsibility to perform taken to a higher personal level, and (4) accountability for performance that is seen as beneficial. When people collectively work beyond participation, there is a flow to how they work together, making high productivity and innovation possible, even probable.

Whereas in the past participation was initiated or offered to the tested few by management, membership designates it as assumed for all members, no matter where they work. Each member acknowledges that competence and top performance are virtually everywhere in the workplace community. This concept stimulates enrollment in the organizational purpose, facilitates member acceptance of shared urgency of performance, and expands opportunities for contribution and success for the individual, group, and organization.

When members work beyond participation, the authority to act and the right to perform address issues of power. The first power role is *position power.* Position addresses status, title, and whom one reports to. In the hierarchical organization, position power facilitates the question, Does this person have the right to make this decision or Where is he or she on the organizational chart? In the Membership Organization, title, status, and whom the member reports to are incidental. Position power may be temporary and based in the moment: Right at this moment, what this person is performing is significant. The core leader in the organization may, for this moment, be heeding the leadership position of someone at the edge of the circle. Position power takes on a meaning of *role power.*

The second power role is *task power,* suggesting that expertise in what I am doing is a powerful employability concept in the Membership Organization. How I work, what task tactics I use to do my job well, and whether I ask challenging questions will affect my task performance power on the job. When others are looking for someone to innovate or answer questions, task power matters—no matter what job I am doing.

The third power role is *personal power.* In the healthy, productive individual, personal power is the ability to balance and direct creative energy in directions that affect personal and workplace community performance. It includes the key elements of confidence, decisiveness, control, skills, and awareness (personal, political, and organizational)—issues of employability in the workplace of today (LaBella & Leach, 1983, 1985). Personal power is also based on the motivational factors of competence, empowerment, challenge, and significance discussed in Chapter Three.

The fourth power role is *relationship power.* Relationship power relates to the member's ability to connect to others. Informal leaders often are high in personal power. The ability to influence, facilitate, contribute, and work beyond participation is a part of relationship power. The ability of community to change is often dependent on having credible members available with high levels of relationship power.

The final power is *knowledge power.* In most organizations, the "learning center" is an important ingredient to member and organizational success. Knowledge power has in recent decades taken on new significance and meaning. Knowledge changes things. The right person with the right knowledge can reduce complexity. Knowledge is powerful—no matter what role you play or where you are in the organizational circle.

Although most members see participation as beneficial, non-participation can also exist, based on fear, anger, mistrust, reluctance, doubt, and disinterest. *Fear* occurs when members have learned that deep participation exposes them to risks they do not want to take. *Anger* is a response to feelings of past victimization, injustice, or isolation. *Mistrust* is the result of inconsistent, unreliable, noncredible leadership whose actions often fail to reflect verbal invitations to participate. *Reluctance* indicates a wait-and-see stance regarding deep participation. *Doubt* suggests that the member has limited faith in the benefit of expanded participation. *Disinterest* tells observers that there is no ownership or enrollment in improving decisions, processes, and productivity in the work. Getting past these six barriers requires a new focus on top performance and the establishment of a safe environment where deeper participation becomes the norm.

Membership takes participation and involvement to a higher level. In contrast to the old mind-set of following, membership includes the sharing of knowledge and innovation (thinking) and the use of the talents and skills (doing) of all members, making it possible for them to connect and participate across all levels of the workplace community. Organizations can no longer afford to separate the doers from the thinkers. The new mind-set recognizes that leading and following are no longer divided into separate functions; *all members share in the responsibility of running successful organizations*. For this reason, working beyond participation across blurred lines is essential to sustaining and expanding individual, group, and organizational achievement.

The Role of Leaders

Of course, formal, selected leaders do still lead. Every organization has designated decision makers and vision creators who are alert to the trends of the external environment. In the Membership Organization, leader-members understand that there are members in diverse roles in the organization who can contribute to vision creation and decision making. For this reason, the leader-members actively seek out, listen to, and act on the input and vision of their co-members at all levels.

Following still exists, but in different, highly active, and collaborative ways. Formal leaders, in their co-member roles, routinely turn leadership activities over to informal leader-members when appropriate. The role of the informal leader is considered a normal function of all co-members—regardless of their formal level of performance. Members routinely assume the leader-member role of coaching new members. New skills must be learned from recognized experts—wherever they exist. These experts may be peers or subordinates who become the leader in training the new group member. Leaders also routinely turn leadership of projects over to members who have the knowledge to lead the project to success. The leader who steps back, turning responsibility over to co-members, is acknowledging the talents and expertise of others across the circle.

The Membership Organization stimulates top performance, growth, and the achievement of a value-added status for the members and the organization as a whole. This represents the basis for re-enrollment, pride, and deep participation in the workplace community. Organizational growth (and survival) happens when members *want* to do the best job they can, and when they *want* to ask internal and external customers the questions that open doors to innovation and renewal: How can I help you do your job well, and how can I serve you better? A sense of urgency and feelings of pride activate high-quality relationships built over time. Urgency and pride initiate member motivation to nurture the interpersonal activities that establish relational connections across the organization.

In this atmosphere, organization and member mind-sets move to a higher level of acceptance and involvement. Members are the organization and as such are the catalyst for the establishment of this new, high-performing mind-set.

Co-Construction of the Organization

Organizations do not "just happen," nor do they develop by accident. Rather, organizational members purposefully design them. Diana Whitney, an organizational consultant in Taos, New Mexico, says, "It's our concepts and assumptions about being human that we use consciously and unconsciously as design criteria for the organizations we create" (Personal communication, 1995). Members design their organizations around what is valued, what is accepted (and constructed) as truth, what is assumed as appropriate and acceptable, and what influences individuals and the group. How the members do business and the business conditions created through their actions evolve because organizations and their members are evolutionary—ever changing into new personal and organizational realities. Members at all levels constantly collaborate (whether they want to or not) in a process of changing (or retaining) opinions, mindsets, and visions of the work world (Menken, 1988).

All members together construct their organization. In an interview, Peter Block (1995, p. 4) said, "It took a lot of subordinates not wanting responsibility to create the system we have." Without the permission, enthusiasm, and cooperation of their members, organizations cannot become top performers. How the workplace community works together is significant to the evolutionary process of becoming a peak organization in the present and the future. Organizations are co-constructions of participants.

The environments of organizations are "constructed" by the processes, procedures, and communication interactions designed by the participants. The hierarchical, controlling organization occurs based on the control actions of the top management and the compliance responses of "followers." Over time, this scenario of "how to be accepted as a good performer," when unchallenged, creates a formal, distant culture of problem-based relationship across the organization. In the more open, participative organization, informality, innovation, and challenge (questioning and informing) are accepted as the way to work successfully, while formal systems of work practices provide needed structure and support for the participative environment to perform (McLagan & Nel, 1996). Entrepreneurial, participative interchanges and activities are more able to flourish, encouraging creative, energized actions of partnership and contribution.

When an autocratic, hierarchical organization attempts to move to teams, it is up to the leaders to take the first steps toward change. In one organization seeking change, invitations to make decisions were rejected because of past negative experiences of disempowerment when spontaneous action was taken. The leadership initiated education and training, support, and encouragement, while actively turning over authority and accountability for making decisions within the areas of expertise of the members. Instead of punishing members for not making decisions or for making the wrong decisions, the leader coached, sponsored, and worked with the members in decision-making activities. The leaders actively asked for suggestions and input, both individually and in group meetings, sharing information that was previously seen as "not understandable" by the members. The process created partnerships across formerly solid boundaries of status and power. The new way of working established rapport, connection, and the acceptance previously seen as impossible, even inappropriate, across the organization. This organization tapped the resources and knowledge of all members to, over time, co-construct a new organization.

The successful Membership Organization can be constructed when the *organizational stance* and individual *member stance* coincide and demonstrate an overall viewpoint of acceptance and inclusion. This worldview indicates a mind-set of co-construction, designing new understandings of the stance or worldview that builds a Membership Organization (see Chart 3).

The phrase "all members are constructing the workplace community together" becomes a shared mind-set. When this mind-set is in place, developing successful external customer relationships is easier because it is done as a team that is working toward shared goals. Developing and sustaining internal partnering relationships is also easier because members understand the role of co-members as contributing to the success of all members and the workplace community.

CHART 3 Co-Construction of the Organization	
The Organizational Stance	The Member Stance
The organization strives to provide a more open, involved, and supportive atmosphere for a more level working community. The members understand that they are the organization—no matter where they work in the community. As a community, all members are envisioned as credible, willingly responsible, and accountable. Members at all levels individually and collectively contribute to the success and welfare of their organization.	If the company succeeds, each member succeeds. It is appropriate that each member willingly performs as a knowledgeable contributor. To do so requires each member to actively learn and apply skills and abilities and to demonstrate attitudes inside and outside the organization that will enhance opportunities for the company to be a value-added member of their industry and their community. Whether it be from a bench, a desk, or a vehicle, what a member does makes a difference.

All members are constructing the workplace community together.

The Organizational Climate

In the past, organizations laid the responsibility for the climate of the organization at the feet of the leaders. If the climate was less than pleasant, *they* were to blame. There was a lot of finger pointing and asking questions about what *they* were going to do about this place—"Working here stinks." In a membership environment, all members share in the responsibility of creating an interdependent, relational place to work, of attending to "how it feels to work here."

Of course, the who, what, where, why, and how in the workplace community can add to or detract from the climate of the organization and the opportunity to internalize the membership principles. Aspects of these categories include power and connections, identity, capabilities, environment, behaviors, and history.

Who

Power and connections touch on the *who* of the Membership Organization. Membership is a connecting process that activates power and authority throughout the organization. The actual "power people" are not located at specific status levels. Initiation and approval of innovation and performance do not necessarily start in the traditional "thinking" location of the organization—at the "top." When thinking happens throughout the community, power is diffused and connections create learning, acting, and responsibility opportunities for members at all levels.

Identity tells *who* members are in the organization, creating a sense of self and of where each member fits into the organizational picture. It identifies roles and provides a sense of value added, allowing members to identify with the overall mission of the organization. In a highly hierarchical, bureaucratic organization, identity is tied to where members are (or are not) on the organizational chart, the tasks they perform, their ability to "control," and the title of the person they report to. In the Membership Organization, where status lines and boundaries of participation are blurred and members are encouraged, supported, and challenged to contribute, members can retain and expand their sense of identity and connection with the organizational purpose regardless of their position.

What and How

Capabilities of members in the community are critical to personal and organizational achievement and are built on actions of learning taken by individual and group members. Capability expands the *what* and *how* of the organization. Ongoing activities of formal or informal peer training stimulate accomplishment, "connection," and partnership between community members. Membership activities, employability, and learning become self-generated expectations, serving as catalysts for individual members to assume active participation in the organization's growth and achievement.

Where

Environment is a strong influence on whether membership happens and whether it can be sustained over time. Environment involves the *where* of the Membership Organization and how it may or may not influence reactions. Reactions to the physical working environment can open or close doors to achieving top performance because they are viewed as signals indicating whether members are valued as contributors. The decision makers' willingness or unwillingness to deal with things that are dirty, messy, not working, obsolete, unsafe, or uncomfortable, whether physical or psychological, is a signal of respect or disrespect toward the organizational member. In the Membership Organization, there is an awareness of the members' sense of pride and it is recognized—and communicated—that the work environment matters.

Why

Behaviors are actions or reactions that demonstrate how members feel about their community and the environment they work in every day on the job. This is the *why* of membership. The "I am here voluntarily" aspect of membership disappears when member behaviors indicate they are captive in their jobs. Members justify behavior and performance on the job through choices and perceptions that activate positive or negative responses. In the Membership Organization, members have a sense of responsibility for their own actions; they understand that what they do matters and that their words and actions can directly or indirectly affect the human, social, and financial bottom lines of the organization.

Beliefs and values that are congruent with individual, group, and organizational accomplishment are basic to the achievement of top performance in the workplace community. Personal beliefs and values, and whether they do or do not coincide with organizational beliefs and values, are the why of what is done on the job. They motivate the individual to perform (or not perform), and they verify internal "permission" regarding behavior on the job. Member beliefs and values reinforce or detract from the membership concept as well as from the members' willingness to enroll in the workplace community.

History is a powerful influence on the present and future of the organization and its community of members. Organizations do not become what they are or design how the members work together overnight. There is an evolutionary process that creates a culture built on people spending time together, sharing common uncertainties, and learning how to cope with those uncertainties together. What evolves is a unique history of a particular community of people who have learned how to deal with, as Trice and Beyer (1993) note, "a unique set of physical, social, political, and economic circumstances" where "these ideas and practices begin to have a kind of life of their own" (p.6). Thus looking at historical memories of the organization can offer an added understanding of the *why* of community behavior. Of course, there is a pull of the past that makes it difficult to create a new direction or a new way of working. The culture and climate of the historical organization influence the ability of the organization to commit to and persevere in a Membership Organization environment that is more adaptable, less structured, less hierarchical, and less bureaucratic.

The Principles of Membership

Certain principles and language significant to the way things work in the Membership Organization serve as guideposts to stimulate the growth and achievement of a value-added status for the members and the organization. The principles or guideposts address issues of contribution, motivation, decisioning, relationship, leadership, accountability, and advocacy.

The Principles of Membership, when accepted as the way to work throughout the organization, encourage members to share a common purpose, vision, and goals; stimulate interactive energy; and create the possibility that members can and will accept the urgency of performance as a personal responsibility. These seven principles form the structural framework for the remaining chapters of the book.

Summary

Membership, as applied in the workplace community, is an individual and organizational shift—a mind-set of acceptance and

The Principles of Membership

Contribution All organizational participants are "members." All members, wherever they are in the organizational circle, contribute to the well-being of their co-members and the workplace community.

Motivation Members (1) are *competent* to perform, (2) are *challenged* to perform, (3) are personally and collectively *empowered* to take action, and (4) feel they and their work are *significant* to the overall achievement of the organization.

Decisioning Decisions are made in the organization through consideration of the three bottom lines: human, social, and financial. The identification of potential long-term outcomes for the organization, as well as for the internal and external customers and the community, are central to the decisioning process.

Relationship For all members, the "relational approach" is basic in working with others. It is the responsibility of every member to establish connecting relationships that work and that add energy to the individual, the group, and the organization.

Leadership Chosen, assigned leader-members still lead. Leadership happens at all levels, and every member has the potential to be a catalyst for achievement and an agent for change.

Accountability Members are willingly and individually responsible and accountable for working toward organizational goals.

Advocacy Member willingness to promote co-members and the workplace community positively influences the performance of individuals, groups, and the organization.

inclusion that starts with leader-members. It is also a way to work that requires fll enrollment by members throughout the workplace community, front door to back door, upstairs and downstairs, inside and outside. It is emphatically true that each person, wherever he or she works in the community, makes a difference. It is also true that working in an environment every day in which new outlooks are not accepted as appropriate, even looked on as weak or soft, is painful for members. For this reason, introducing and believing in the Membership Organization as a concept may require determination and courage on the part of the change agent.

Member connections, beliefs, and values must involve inclusion and acceptance, high performance standards, and moving everyone from being just an employee to being a member who achieves top performance—getting beyond participation. A positive, optimistic view encourages and invites deep participation because everyone has something of value to contribute to the welfare of the organization. It is within this premise that the language and Principles of Membership sustain willing, involved members in expanding the three bottom lines of the workplace community.

Courage and determination will be needed to relentlessly move communities to the new "voluntary" community. Srivastva, Fry, and Cooperrider (1990) suggest that leadership is a search through human processes of knowledge, relationship, and action that set highest standards to be used to nourish the social connections of groups and organizations. In the past, members were treated as machinelike (Gergen, 1990). It was thought that feelings and sensitivities could be trained. Connection was not noteworthy. Perceptions of members, good or bad, were based on behavior that was never forgotten. People did not readily accept that changing the environment from one of shaming and blaming to one of accepting and appreciating could make a difference. The successful leader of the future not only will believe so but will take steps to bring about a new workplace community that nurtures the Membership Organization.

This book is a conceptual framework that builds on the work of David Noer and others. Nevertheless, some will say that the Membership Organization is impossible, unachievable, illogical, even irresponsible. Even so, it is suggested that you set aside judgment and read in terms of challenging the taken-for-granted and being open to new ways of working effectively together. Members and their organizations have the potential to perform far beyond what has been seen or expected in the past. For this reason, the following chapters, while focused on the Principles of Membership, include shifts to new perspectives that can provide the opportunity for expanded performance, which will increase all members' desires to re-enroll in their workplace communities.

Among top-performing co-members in a Membership Organization, certain attitudes prevail regarding contribution, motivation, decision-making leadership, relationship, accountability, and advocacy. Think about your personal "membership stance" and your workplace community's "organizational stance" around the Principles of Membership (see pages 19 and 23). The following two assessment questionnaires offer you an opportunity to pre-evaluate your organization and your own personal perspectives on the Principles. Covered in the Personal Membership Performance Rating Form (see pages 28 and 29) are certain attitudes (values) that are seen as vital to being a top-performing member in a membership-based organization. These same performance attitudes are addressed from a collective, organizational, communitywide perspective in the Membership Organization Rating Form (see pages 26 and 27). The following chapters individually address the Principles of Membership. In preparation, I encourage you to think clearly and honestly about the ratings on the scale from 1 ("never") to 5 ("always"). Being overly generous or underperceptive can cloud your awareness of your personal or organizational stance. Scoring instructions are included at the bottom of each rating form.

The Membership Organization Rating Form

The following questions offer an opportunity to rate the performance of your workplace community as a Membership Organization. To the right of each question write the most appropriate number from the following scale:

1 Never   2 Seldom   3 Sometimes   4 Frequently   5 Always

Membership

1. My workplace community encourages members at all levels to actively participate in achieving the goals of the organization. _____

2. My community functions in ways that are beneficial to its members as well as to its customers. _____

Contribution

3. Most members in my community believe that, for the most part, people want to do a good job. _____

4. Most members have a sense of urgency regarding the success of the workplace community. _____

Motivation

5. Members are motivated to exert high levels of energy in their work. _____

6. The workplace community demonstrates that each person's performance is valued. _____

Decisioning

7. When decisions are made, consideration is given to their long-term impact on human, social, and financial outcomes. _____

8. Decisions are made with the participation of those members who do the work. _____

Relationship

9. The organization encourages informal, interactive relationships. _____

10. There are many examples of effective formal and informal partnerships across the workplace community. _____

Leadership

11. Our leaders are positive models for how to work well together. _____

12. Members at all levels are encouraged to assume active leadership. _____

Accountability

13. Accountability for workplace community performance is distributed across the organization.   _____

14. Our leaders encourage members to take responsibility for learning new skills.   _____

Advocacy

15. The external community sees this organization as a good corporate citizen.   _____

16. There are many examples of members striving to nurture a positive work climate.   _____

Total   _____

The Membership Organization Scores

65–80: You have a Membership Organization. This mind-set has made it possible to purposefully blur the lines of title and status, creating a climate in which acting on input from members at all levels is the way work is accomplished. All members are vital to the growth of the workplace community, and the members are energized by expanded possibilities in the future for themselves and for their community.

49–64: This community is a good place to work, but it is not yet a high-achieving Membership Organization. For the most part, members can work together across lines of titles and status, but there are still difficult barriers to working together at a deeper level. Change agents within the organization are seeking ways to move to deeper levels of member participation.

33–48: The community is struggling and is sensing a need for change. There is an awareness throughout the organization that new, more successful ways of working are possible. This creates the potential for moving toward becoming a Membership Organization, but those who sense this possibility feel lost as to where to begin.

16–32: Bringing up the concept of membership would be a good way to get a cynical laugh in this organization. Many members feel discouraged, depressed and discounted—and rightly so. It will require a major change effort in this organization to create hope of becoming a higher-performing Membership Organization.

Personal Membership Performance Rating Form

The following questions offer an opportunity to examine your personal actions of membership based on the parameters of the Membership Organization. To the right of each question, record your perception of your own actions of membership within your workplace community using the following scale:

1 Never   2 Seldom   3 Sometimes   4 Frequently   5 Always

Membership
1. I am responsible for my own achievement as well as for the achievement of my organization. _____

2. I am empowered to take action as a representative of my organization. _____

Contribution
3. I put forth my best effort because my work makes a difference in the overall achievement of the workplace. _____

4. I work *with*, not for, the leaders in my workplace community. _____

Motivation
5. I continually challenge myself to grow in my work. _____

6. I seek opportunities to take responsibility for my work. _____

Decisioning
7. I am willing to make tough choices when difficult decisions must be made. _____

8. I actively seek needed information from others at all levels in order to make good decisions. _____

Relationship
9. I work well with others in my community. _____

10. I participate in successful partnerships that contribute to individual and organizational achievement. _____

Leadership
11. I assume a leadership role when needed. _____

12. I positively influence others regarding workplace initiatives. _____

Accountability

13. I take responsibility for issues on which I want to have an impact.   _____

14. I ask questions and actively seek answers when I am concerned about workplace issues.   _____

Advocacy

15. I promote my co–members as capable, contributing members of the organization.   _____

16. I am a positive representative of this community.   _____

Total   _____

Personal Membership Scores

65–80:   Congratulations! You have a Membership mind-set. But don't get overly confident. To work from a Membership stance means you must be constantly vigilant to the Principles in determining how to work with your co-members and you must be aware of the need to personally contribute to sustaining the Membership mind-set in the workplace community.

49–64:   You know that a Membership Organization cannot be achieved without your personal understanding of and commitment to the Principles of Membership. For the most part, you are successful in performing from a Membership stance. But you also see that there is more you as an individual can do to make membership possible within the community and to promote greater achievement for yourself and others.

33–48:   You are struggling and feel frustrated with what is happening on the job; but you see some hope in moving toward the Membership way of working and increasing opportunities for innovation and growth. Occasionally you try applying one of the Principles to see what would happen—and see potential. But where do you go from here?

16–32:   You are not operating from a Membership mind-set, and you are a stumbling block for those around you.

2

While there are many constraints on the behavior of individuals in organizations, most of the behavior that is observed is the result of individuals' conscious decisions . . . [about] coming to work, staying at work, and in other ways being a member of the organization . . . [and] about the amount of effort they will direct towards performing their jobs. This includes decisions about how hard to work, how much to produce, at what quality, etc.

David A. Nadler and Edward E. Lawler III, "Motivations: A Diagnostic Approach," *Psychological Dimensions of Organizational Behavior*

Contribution

All organizational participants are "members." All
members, wherever they
are in the organizational
circle, contribute to the
well-being of their co-
members and the work-
place community.

Recently, a manager in a large manufacturing facility attended a dinner held by his company to welcome new management employees. He watched and listened as each new employee stood up and introduced him- or herself as "working for" or "working under" other managers. When that manager's own hiree introduced himself, he made an obvious point of saying that he was *"working with"* his new manager. It was a proud moment for the manager—someone was hearing his message. He was still smiling when he later told the story.

In a successful organizational community, it is understood that the contributions of all members are vital to the success of the organization and that *working with* is different from *working for.* When *working for,* members' minds can become paralyzed eight hours a day. They can choose to only receive; they can respond without ever initiating. It is management's job to tell them what to do and they'll do it, if it doesn't take much effort. They merely put their minds in neutral and cruise. If what managers tell them to do doesn't work, they know whom to blame. It's easy—"I'm a follower."

Working with recognizes abilities, skills, and input. For leader-members, it means collaborating instead of dictating. For all members, it means involvement and ownership instead of telling or reacting. *Working with* encourages learning; merges skills, abilities, and opportunities; and locates member-experts wherever they work in the company. In a more level workplace community, members communicate concerns and share knowledge. They initiate, challenge appropriately, and follow through; they participate in making their organization work—together.

In the old way of working, thinking and doing were performed at different levels of the organization. Upper managers thought of what to do, middle managers facilitated it, and employees did the actual work. In the Membership Organization, all members actively participate in the *thinking* side of organizing by sharing knowledge and identifying innovations that are important to organizational growth and survival. Members also know that, in order for the workplace community to succeed, the *doing* side of organizing must use talents and skills of members at every level of the organization. Working together creates new, innovative products and services and identifies the best way possible to make and deliver those products and services.

Thinking and Doing

The roles of doing and thinking are interactive, not localized or separated, in the Membership Organization. Wherever the member is located who has the greatest ability to do the job, that is where the work is performed. Leader-members now think and do; co-members, wherever they are located, also think and do. These performance and consultative roles make it possible to connect members across all levels of the organization, creating new, innovative partnerships and teams that in the past could not have existed. It is no longer feasible to separate the doers from the thinkers.

Everyone must share in the responsibility of running the organization. Douglas K. Smith (1996) says, "Today, the people in an effective organization must both think and do, both manage others and manage themselves, both make decisions and do real work" (p. 201). It should be stressed that "managing others" applies not just to "management." In order for an organization to be successful in the new environment, members throughout the organization must be willing to lead, managing others in new ways whenever necessary. All members must be consultative and performance oriented—otherwise the possibility of a top-performing organization is limited.

A more level workplace is characterized by less formality, blurred lines of status, and more direct contact with the co-member in the formal leading role. With all members sharing ideals for high performance and responsibility, it is more probable that the leader-member will be working beside the co-member instead of in front directing or behind pushing. A more level structure makes it possible for informal leaders to be spread across the levels and areas of the organization. All levels, whether in a team organization or a traditional organization, are empowered to assume leadership and know they are participants in the achievements (and the failures) of the organization.

The more level working environment is an interdependent, relationship-based arena that pulls all members into an empowered, energized work environment. Actions of empowerment at all levels are encouraged, nurtured, and acknowledged; and possibilities thought of and initiated by members at all levels are examined and considered equally.

Performance Role

Task performance is a role members have always had. Performing well means getting the job done—the normal "doing" role in the company. In the performance role in the Membership Organization, each member (1) is responsible for his or her own level of expertise (learning is a choice); (2) is responsibile for identifying and doing what is expected (and unexpected) and then going beyond that mark to top performance; and (3) performs in ways that contribute to the achievement and growth of the organization, the group, and the individual.

Because they are responsible for their own expertise, members can no longer wait to be told what education and training are needed to do the job well. As the one doing the work, the individual knows what is needed to perform well. It is the member's responsibility to seek information and take advantage of opportunities to learn and increase his or her own employability. This makes it necessary to watch for trends, initiate suggestions and innovations, and risk being seen as not knowing everything about the job. Staying at the task with head down, doing things the same way year after year, is an invitation to obsolescence and being "out of the loop."

Being guardian of one's own employability means putting in after-hours work. If the organization sees no value in gaining or providing additional expertise, yet the member feels that additional knowledge is important both personally and on the job, the effective member seeks it on his or her own. Taking classes, attending seminars, and reading materials that extend individual knowledge take dedication and willingness to work on personal time and at personal expense. Blaming the organization for lack of employability is no longer valid. When organizational funding is not available, investing one's own money can increase performance potential and employability on the job.

Awareness of my own performance potential and employability was significant to my accomplishments in the workplace. Early in my career, while working as the assistant to a CEO in a national organization with several thousand employees, I sought to expand my role. On my own, I began attending university classes in business. Eventually, I had three departments reporting to me. My credibility, salary, satisfaction, and perception of contribution increased.

After this organization relocated, I went to another organization as a secretary to the CEO, but I lost my opportunity to supervise and the credibility I had established as a performer at the previous organization. I continued with my after-hours studies and eventually received a business degree and a master's degree in organization development. With these credentials, I was able to move back into supervision, and I became a customer advocate and marketing representative. I had the opportunity to design programs and to train others. This organization was not routinely innovative, but because of a relational leader, I had opportunities to do behind-the-scenes work. Some leaders in the organization saw my potential and tapped the resource available to them; others discounted my abilities because of my original "less-than" role. Eventually the relational leader left. I spent years doing after-hours work to gain skills and experience in the role that was my goal, hoping that I would be able to use them in my organization. When it became apparent that this organization was not going to use the skills and experience I offered, I decided it was time to move on.

Consultative Role

The addition of the consultative role at all levels makes it possible for everyone to work more effectively. Through the consultative role, members actively contribute to achievement in their own work, the work of their co-members, and the goals of the workplace community. Purposeful thinking and goal-significant doing are now combined, increasing the knowledge available to all in the workplace community.

The consultative role hinges on the members' willingness to provide expertise (while working toward consensus) as informal internal consultants in their individual areas of knowledge and skill. Members who perform as internal consultants also reciprocally learn from those to whom they offer information, thereby adding to their own storehouse of knowledge, which they can then pass on to others.

Effective consultative members set a positive tone in their group; they support, inform, and influence others and are often catalysts for change and survival. They initiate new ideas and respond to the inquiries of other members with new ideas. They take their jobs very seriously, wherever they are in the community.

The consultative member's knowledge and skills are important and may be used often, due to their credibility in the eyes of their co-members. Effective consultative members are usually seen by others as

- Credible in their work and their relationships
- Able to communicate needs and expectations clearly
- Willing to exercise power and authority beyond their title
- Willing to share knowledge and expertise

Being highly visible is not a requirement for a successful consultative member. In many organizations, the quiet, unassuming consultative member—sitting off to the side working while being aware and involved—is highly effective. Such members know what to do when, and they know what *not* to do. They are proud of their work and their organization, and their pride is reflected in how they do their work. Of the five kinds of power—position power, task power, personal power, relationship power, and knowledge power (see Chapter One)—they may very well have four. The one they do not have, and the least important to top performance, is position power. Fortunately, the four they do have result in the most important ingredient of power: *influence*. The outcome is that they are the ones who get things done and to whom people go when they need assistance.

Consultative members connect with their co-members and are usually "other" focused. When they see someone struggling on the job, they help that person. They become consultative members because of their knowledge of the job and their willingness to help others achieve. Their willingness to help is naturally reciprocated when needed.

The consultative role includes the willingness to "pay back what I have received" in positive, productive relationships that support the growth of individuals, groups, and the organizations they represent. Top-performing consultative members make no assumptions that their organization "owes them," and they come in every day to *earn* their pay. Ultimately their attitude communicates their willingness to perform the consultative role, which they know benefits their internal and external customers. The credibility of such members increases, connections are solidified, and the members are seen as beneficial to the organization.

From Competition to Cooperation

Increasingly, organizations are seeking structures that are more participative, where individual responsibility and creativity are emphasized. These organizations want to replace competition with cooperation. Of necessity, organizational communities are recognizing the need for working more "relationally"—making positive exchanges possible by replacing one-way relationships that were less productive and inclusive with interconnecting relationships.

In a large department of a midwestern organization, for example, the leadership group recognized the need for change— and the need for involvement at every level. A past effort had succeeded in rebuilding the work processes of a portion of the division and had improved customer service, but managing was still paternalistic. There were other issues, including a serious unionization effort in a segment of the division where dissatisfaction with stress, routinization, and workload made it a tough place to work. A leadership group was formed, and the group, with input from the entire organization, fine-tuned the values and vision that evolved continuously. Over fifteen months, a 4,500-employee business unit was created and redesigned using the wisdom of frontline employees. The employees did the job redesign. Change process teams were made up of informal leaders from the business unit who were active in valuing, involving, and informing the employees across the business unit. Tom Heuerman, organizational consultant and then division leader of the business unit, says, "We found new meaning in our work. Many of us had never felt more alive or creative. Despite the difficulty of such great change, the employees did not want to return to the old culture, structure, or leadership style. I know, because I asked them—frequently." Without interconnecting relationships that brought members from all levels of the unit into the process, the prospect of accomplishing change while facing potential unionization and other complex work process issues would have been daunting. These new ways of working are successful to the limits of the organization's ability to facilitate them, and often they are more demanding, even more uncomfortable, than originally anticipated. Commenting on the work effort required, Heuerman added, "The work was hard. We made a lot of mistakes and learned from them. The process was often highly stressful because there were many difficult changes to make. People responded. They worked with purpose; they worked hard."

Membership is no different. Although theoretically ideal, the concept of community and the deep participative element of membership prove difficult for many organizations. Status has always been a privilege, even a goal, for management members. The Membership Organization de-emphasizes the levels of "more-thans," disperses power and accountability, and encourages a more level working community in order to tap the talents and skills of members who may have been ignored in the past.

Informal Member-Leadership

Moving beyond participation opens up opportunities for members to contribute at a new level. Wherever expertise is located, leadership can develop. In the past, leadership responsibilities had to be assigned. If leadership was not assigned, co-members waited for leader-members to give their blessings to a member's suggestions and assign a recognized leader to "watch over" the informal leader's work. Then other members would cooperate. Actions viewed as overstepping the bounds, even if performed notably well, meant the member was a potential troublemaker. Not only did the managers take note, the other employees did also. (What makes her think she can tell me what to do? What right does he have to be doing that?)

Choices

In the Membership Organization, all members are potential leaders. Wherever they work, they make conscious or unconscious choices regarding involvement and contribution that may or may not be beneficial to the company and themselves. The choice to lead starts with the *process of noticing* and "refers to the activities of filtering, classifying, and comparing" (Weick, 1995, p. 51). This requires potential leaders to be open to what is going on around them. A machine operator notices a strange noise, slowed response, or heightened scrap rate on his or her machine. A supervisor notices the distraction of a formerly enthusiastic member. The retail associate notices signs of irritation in the demeanor of a customer. The members recognize these messages because of past experience and compare them with accumulated knowledge of what they consider "normal" in that environment. After noticing, members analyze the situation and decide what is to be done: Do they need to tell someone? Can they assume a leadership role and do something right now? Or is it better to wait and see—stay alert to what is happening?

Making a choice and deciding what action to take is significant to empowerment (Kouzes & Posner, 1993), and the willingness to exercise leadership is a personal choice. No matter where members are in the organization, their level of comfort in making choices of leadership and empowerment is dependent on past personal experiences, on observed experiences of others in the organization, on the outcomes of choices made by others, and on the climate of the organization.

Making the "right" choices is related to the ability to understand how results are produced in a particular situation. Of course, there is rarely one right choice; different people choose different alternatives. According to Senge et al. (1994, p. 196), "Choosing is a courageous act: picking the results and actions which you will make into your destiny." When faced with choices, members are saying, I choose to be courageous, I choose to wait, or I choose to use coping strategies and remain helpless. Of course, to choose not to choose is a choice—a potentially bad choice.

Credibility

Informal leadership is an issue of character. The decision to act is based on how members see their work world and on their ability to make clear distinctions about what is happening; it is also based on the priorities of potential informal leaders and their organization, whether they feel their decision will be supported, and the amount of risk involved. Character facilitates these decisions as well as the actions the member will take after decisions are made.

When a member makes the decision *not* to take action when action is appropriate, the member gives value to those who do take action. When action is called for, the choice not to act is an act of self-disempowerment. Even in the past, organizations were built on hidden, unseen decisions by members not inside the inner circle. Peter Block (1995, p. 3) says, "Nothing important ever starts at the top. Most of the things start at the middle, or bottom, and the top catches wind of it and says, 'Let's do this some more.'" This may or may not be a rash statement, but the message is there: Opportunity for tapping the ideas and expertise of members in the organization is a financial and human bottom lines issue. By legitimatizing informal leadership as appropriate and making it an everyday, assumed occurrence, organizations expand responsibility and accountability and uncover new levels of informal leadership and achievement. In the new Membership Organization, informal leaders

- Don't have to be blessed
- Don't have to inherit influence
- Know how to enlist others in their concerns and activities
- Do have to earn the opportunity through motivation, energy, and skills

In the past, members not in the inner circle had to feel safe in order to move willingly into the informal leader role. Safety meant that someone was protecting them and someone was available to give permission. But often informal leaders did not ask for help even when help existed. Asking meant they did not know what they were doing—and that was bad. So they felt vulnerable and helpless, which undermined their willingness to make risky decisions and move beyond the normal way of doing things. Working beyond participation was not possible. They worked within self- and organization-imposed boundaries that limited opportunities to be top-performance members.

Occasionally help was given whether it was wanted or not. The informal leaders reluctantly accepted the help, which sometimes took their work off in a direction that they neither appreciated nor saw as appropriate. They felt disempowered and resentful. The message was, You can't do this without me. To avoid disempowerment, (1) the member must be willing to *ask for help and be clear about what is needed;* and (2) the formal leader-member must *provide help on the member's terms.* Supportive coaching is different from helping and is entirely appropriate.

The message is clear: Especially in the early stages of the Membership Organization, leader-members may need to exercise great patience, understanding, and noticing to stay in tune with the members' signals of confidence or lack of confidence in their own decisions. Leaders must early on encourage actions of self-empowerment—allowing mistakes and providing support that is sincere and freely given. It is during this time that leader-members gain credibility and acceptance (legitimacy) in their ability to lead in the more level workplace circle.

The Courageous Member

Value-added members in the Membership Organization are courageous and have qualities that demonstrate their willingness to use their strengths productively as top performers (see Chart 4). Is there one best formula for being a good member? No. But the positive, contributing member of a Membership Organization has certain characteristics. He or she:

Considers the needs of co-members and customers. Membership expands the individual's role in the success of others in the organization. It also directly or indirectly affects everyone's opportunities and abilities to gain information and learn from each other. By seeking deeper involvement in the success of others, the member connects to the needs of others, creating "partnerships" that enhance everyone's performance.

Challenges appropriately and constructively. Members can contribute significantly to the success of the organization. Challenging means asking tough questions, providing information, seeking explanations, and successfully integrating the organizational purpose. Authentic, constructive, and deep participation of members at all levels in testing and confirming the processes and goals of the organizational community result in organizational growth and survival.

Connects to the group and organization represented. Connections are based on a motivation to be tied to the needs and aspirations of a co-member or group. When the relationship is internalized, each member becomes a representative of the connection; a partnership is formed. Both parties have a positive orientation toward the partnership and what it represents. Positive connections survive even though the connection is made with a person, group, or organization that is vulnerable, imperfect, and even demanding.

Contributes responsible solutions. The successful member knows the purpose and goals of the organization, making it possible to notice when "something is wrong here." These actions of "noticing" support the member's responsibility to identify needs, solutions, innovations, and customer concerns. Regardless of the size of the organization or his or her position within it,

CHART 4   The Courageous Member

■ *Considers* the needs of co-members and customers

■ *Challenges* appropriately and constructively

■ *Connects* to the group and organization represented

■ *Contributes* responsible solutions

■ *Commits* to following through

■ *Continually* uses patience in the process

■ *Catches* the fever of the organization

■ *Celebrates* accomplishments genuinely and appropriately

■ *Conveys* positive observations and advocacy viewpoints

the member understands that *each person is the organization and can contribute to solving problems.*

Commits to following through. The extent of a member's contribution is measured by his or her willingness to follow through when opportunities occur. Being involved and then following through when needed increases respect, confirms commitment, and provides opportunities for the member and the group to contribute. Following through effectively may require the member to ask for help or require others to offer help when needed.

Continually uses patience in the process. Not everything or everyone works perfectly; patience and perseverance may be required. The leader-member may need to schedule "learning events" for co-members. Members may not automatically understand their role in the new organizational community—education, training, nurturing, and sustenance of the process will require patience by all members of the organization.

Catches the fever of the organization. Catching the fever requires enthusiasm, enrollment, and forgiveness. The successful member stretches to meet the challenges of the new community, understanding that putting energy into the new reality of membership by all members is essential for success.

Celebrates accomplishments genuinely and appropriately. Many observers scoff at loud pronouncements of success. Every change has an obvious downside. The Membership Organization will create fears of loss and of increased involvement. Nevertheless, celebrations of involvement and accomplishment and recognition of those who are willing to be pioneers in the process are important—but must be appropriate. Leaders know that many who accept the new way of working will hide, seeking to make small, incremental changes while working with the willing and the unwilling. Such members take small, quiet steps toward the new way of working, winning over with nurturing perseverance those who are reluctant. These members will not always be easy to find, but they will be the ones who actually bring about change. By only recognizing those who are most obvious (often those in the inner circle), leaders cause the quieter ones to feel less significant. Leaders should take heed when celebrating and pay attention to the quiet but active members.

Conveys positive observations and advocacy viewpoints. The successful member is a cheerleader for the organization. He or she advocates the organization to others, who realize that this member knows best the truth about this organization because of working there. Each member can positively or negatively affect an organization's success by what he or she says and does—on and off the job—as will be discussed further in Chapter Eight.

Uniqueness and Individuality

An organizational atmosphere that encourages innovation, creativity, and uniqueness supports survival in the turbulence of today's organizational environment. Hanging on to unique characteristics and individuality is important. Unique characteristics of individual members contribute to an organization's ability to adjust and be flexible.

Criticism of individuality and uniqueness, whether given openly or covertly, is threatening and potentially degrading. Discounting attempts to retain unique characteristics causes individuals to challenge those who demand conformity. It is appropriate that members be asked to forgo disruptive, inappropriate group behaviors. The question is, how disruptive and how inappropriate are those behaviors? In the past, organizations demonstrated rigid expectations for success in the workplace.

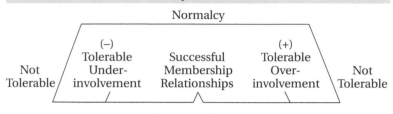

CHART 5   Model of Normalcy and Tolerance

These expectations resulted in signals of approval or disapproval that were divisive and limiting. Favoritism was obvious or assumed when exceptions were made. Strengthened involvement and connections in the Membership Organization widen the realm of the acceptable. Increased tolerance allows members to retain uniqueness and individuality.

Membership increases the vulnerability of all members, from the core to the outer edges of the expanded circle. New freedom to make decisions, opportunities to have real input and attention will be frightening at first. In order to sustain the process, relationships must build on a shared vision of the future. The narrow ranges of "normalcy" of involvement are gone forever. The Membership Organization tolerates, even expects and encourages, individuality and differences, deep participation and the complexities that go with it. Occasionally leader-members feel their co-members are overinvolved but the co-members disagree and continue to be involved. Occasionally leader-members feel co-members are underinvolved but the members disagree and continue to not be involved. Within the "tolerable" to "not tolerable" range, open dialogue and acceptance as well as coaching and connection prevail (see Chart 5). Toleration of the "under" and "over" requires members to view individuality as beneficial. In recent years organizations have moved or hired "non-traditionals" (females and minorities) into previously "male" positions. Tolerance is strained, but in most cases, the resulting diversity brings new acceptance and appreciation of uniqueness and individuality.

In the old way of doing business, members working in the white spaces of the organizational chart—the doers—were not seen as individuals; they were extensions of their "doing." Toleration and coaching of those who were over- or underinvolved was limited. They were faceless and replaceable. (As a manager said in regard to a request for a pay increase for an employee, "She's easily replaced. If she doesn't like her salary, don't let the door hit her in the ass on the way out.") In the past, members who took the risk of sharing concerns or information about their work were looked on as "different" by their peers. They had actually thought things through enough to give intelligent feedback, and worst of all, they wanted to tell someone! Often the manager would take those intelligent words and turn them into his or her own—and get the credit for the member's information. "Employees" expected such treatment. "Toleration" was expected by the less-thans.

Now leaders know that their co-members are no longer willing to be treated as mindless less-thans. Also leaders now know that their co-members are important to the organization's ability to achieve in the marketplace. As individuals, top-performing members make a difference. Whether they are positive, proactive members of the organization or negative, passive employees, they add to or detract from the performance of the organizational community. As individuals, members must be responsible for what they do and how they do it—and for whether they are positive or negative. After all, they make a difference in their organizations.

To illustrate the concept, let me describe my three highly individual children. Terri, a conscientious, other-focused nurse, works in an alternative birthing center in a large hospital. She is a list maker and sustains her husband, three kids, and organized lifestyle with her never-ending lists. My second child, Michael, is an innovative risk taker, entrepreneur, and challenger of the normal. Specializing in public affairs, he travels widely and is active in political campaigns, and at this writing he is living and working in Russia with his new Russian wife. He does not maintain lists—it takes too much time away from the action he is creating. My youngest, daughter Stacy, is a traffic engineer and different from the other two—she takes *calculated* risks; she likes to travel for fun and is reluctantly willing to limit her travel opportunities within the confines of a job she enjoys. She makes lists only when she really has to.

If I had attempted to put my three children into a mold, not one of them would have fit—they are wonderfully different. And

I pity any organization that tries to mold them into organizational clones. Each has a gift to give, each is different from the other, and each makes things work in his or her own way. That is how the successful workplace works—by allowing individuals to fit themselves into a working model while independently and interdependently achieving. It can be exciting and grueling for everyone involved.

Dependence, Counterdependence, Independence, and Interdependence

Geoffrey Bellman (1992) discusses *power positions,* which are a progression of *dependence, counterdependence, independence,* and *interdependence.* These power positions are significant to an individual's success on the job. Each power position is a result of the individual's emotional response to the situation he or she is experiencing. A given position indicates feelings of control or lack of control, fear and hope. How individuals work and relate to those around them, what they say and do, reveals these emotional positions. The dependent person rarely questions; the counterdependent person aggressively questions everything—to the wrong people; the independent person and the interdependent person question as needed.

Personal mastery includes a progression through stages of dependence, counterdependence, exclusive and inclusive independence, and interdependence, as seen in Chart 6. The personal mastery continuum divides the segments between two levels of mastery, reliance on others and personal mastery.

Dependence-oriented members insist that someone take care of them—"*You* tell *me* what to do" and "*I'll* do whatever you say and ask you no questions." Dependence-oriented people want and expect support, but too much support actually increases their dependence (Kouzes & Posner, 1993). Dependent persons may be high contributors (afraid not to be). Dependence also happens when they are happy with "doing just enough." Such dependent people are often the mediocre employees who say, "Don't be in front and don't be in back, stay in the middle where they won't notice you. Only do enough to keep the check coming," or "I do what I'm told, that's all they can ask."

CHART 6   The Personal Mastery Continuum

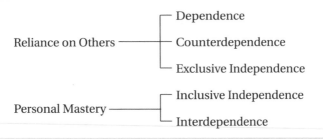

Reliance on Others ——— ┌ Dependence
                       ├ Counterdependence
                       └ Exclusive Independence

Personal Mastery ——— ┌ Inclusive Independence
                     └ Interdependence

Dependence is

- Willingly doing the same things the same way every day
- Working where you *have* to, not where you *want* to
- Complaining and not offering information to people who can do something about problems
- Keeping your head down, keeping quiet, and hoping for the best

Psychologically healthy employees do not want to remain dependent. Ideally, normal life cycles move us toward independence and to active applications of interdependence. Practiced dependence limits our opportunities to even occasionally act independently, resulting in frustration and feelings of hopelessness and helplessness—and then cynicism prevails.

When people are put on pedestals, they may not reach their potential. They may fear that those of us worshipping from below will not like it if they falter. Nor can they be what others expect them to be—perfect. They inevitably fall from their pedestals with a resounding thump and others feel betrayed. When trust and respect are dependent on perfection, the betrayed may turn to mistrust and disrespect.

The *counterdependent* practitioner is the perpetual rebel who focuses on *you—You* didn't do what you were supposed to do; *you* made it hard for me; *you* weren't there when I needed you; *you* are the one I blame for this. In the workplace, this person is not willing to accept decision-making responsibility—*You* really don't want me to make decisions, and anyway *you* will not like the decisions I make. Blaming is this person's game. He or she is perpetually in a reactive stance, wanting to have power and responsibility but constantly blaming others for not providing the opportunities. The counterdependent practitioner, who feels helpless, hopeless, and unworthy, has a cynical outlook.

Exclusive independence-oriented people focus on *I*—*I* take full responsibility; *I* will make it work; *I* can do it by myself; *I* want to look good alone. Control is the name of the game. Exclusive independent people like to do things on their own and yet sometimes wish for the support and input of others. Yet when attempting to partner, they are surprised when people are reluctant to work with them because of previous experiences. Such people accept challenges, "go for the gold," and take risks.

Exclusive independence is a form of dependence when it is based on feelings of suspicion and mistrust and a desire for separation from others. Exclusive independent people may not fit in with a team environment because their suspicion of others makes it impossible for them to work well in a cohesive group. By insisting on being independent, they automatically limit their opportunities to create rapport, give and receive support, and achieve connection in their peer group. By isolating themselves, they are putting up barriers that may limit their ability to perform to the best of their ability. Their actions may also be coping strategies to avoid being vulnerable to group expectations of inclusion and performance they fear cannot be met. Thus, they are still reliant on the approval of others.

The personal mastery stage of the continuum includes *inclusive independence*—the *I and we* stance: *I* can do things on my own while *we* work well as a team to achieve our mutual goals and the goals of the organization. These members work well on their own but seek the input and support of the group when needed. They can be depended on to make appropriate decisions; they have connected with their co-members and know what, how, where, and why things are happening in the team within the boundaries of a realistic need-to-know framework. They are good representatives of their group when they work on their own. Working effectively as an empowered partner includes the responsibility to make decisions that are in line with the goals of the group. Always seeking approval or constantly running to keep the team informed of trivia is disempowering and lowers opportunities for goal attainment. Once members are empowered, they just do it.

The *interdependence* orientation focuses on *we—we* can do it; *we* can work together; *we* can create and construct something together (Covey, 1989). Interdependence relies on relational connections and exchanges that support the tasks on which the group is focusing. Work roles in the workplace are all, to some degree, interdependent and relational. For example, as a leader-member, I influence organizational members to put energy into doing their work. As an accountant, I get information from others so that reports can be finished on time. As a trainer, I connect to the groups I am working with to facilitate their learning opportunities. As an organizational representative to our customers (internal and external), I connect to get the job done in ways that influence customer perceptions of the group I represent and our company. Interdependent exchanges help individual members and their workplace community because members are actively performing their consultative and performance roles.

Summary

Working in a more level community anticipates moving beyond current participation to involvement of individual members at a new level. This involvement represents a paradigm shift for many organizations and their members, and the commitment leader-members make is vital to meeting the challenge.

The barriers against working in new ways may be significant for members at all levels—and lowering them may require all members to make major changes in work habits and attitudes. Commitment to merging inclusive independence and interdependence, which increases opportunities for members to achieve competence, empowerment, challenge, and significance in their work, starts when leadership spreads to the edges of the circle. Hidden skills, knowledge, and abilities are waiting to be tapped for achievement of the community's goals. True interactive dialogue leads the Membership Organization closer to solutions that enhance the bottom lines. These inclusive activities provide opportunities for the Membership Organization to construct new truths for working successfully together.

3

We operate as though perfect
performance is normal and all
else is the exception and deserves
to be complained about. . . . But
organizations don't work. We need
assumptions that support a human
level of performance.

Geoffrey Bellman,
The Consultant's Calling

Motivation

Members (1) are *competent* to perform, (2) are *challenged* to perform, (3) are personally and collectively *empowered* to take action, and (4) feel they and their work are *significant* to the overall achievement of the organization.

It is inevitable and normal that everyone, when working in an organization, feels some love, some hate, and some indifference toward co-members and the organization. The intensity and direction of these feelings vary with the ups and downs of organization life (Leavitt, 1972). Members traditionally assumed their work world would be a rose garden. They assumed wrong. There are thorns in the garden under those pretty roses. Everyone involved must take ownership and consciously stretch to new levels of performance to reach a new way of successfully working together.

Working communities are not perfect because people are not perfect. As a result, even meaningful work can include incidents of disillusionment. Perceptions of jobs and interpersonal relationships on the job affect whether these periods of disillusionment are temporary or permanent.

Leader-members cannot lead a cadre of disillusioned co-members to top performance. Nor can a workplace community achieve when it has a codependent workforce. Getting past codependence requires member enrollment and ownership of the organizational purpose. Relationships and processes require work.

On-the-job relationships that work are caring, respectful, tolerant, and supportive. Members see one another as capable, credible, and contributing. Relationships that do not work are uncaring, disrespectful, intolerant, nonsupportive, and result in degradation and alienation. These attitudes signify that members are valued and trusted—or mistrusted, watched, penalized, and controlled.

Positive feelings and attitudes nurture a high degree of interdependence among co-members. Sharing mutual goals, accepting higher levels of responsibility, and contributing expertise and knowledge to work accountabilities are the result of positive feelings and attitudes.

A positive environment makes working together more comfortable. Personal commonality in the workplace is less important than shared goals collectively and individually seen as worthwhile, attainable, pleasurable, and reasonable. In this atmosphere, trust flourishes and members deal with problems constructively in order to restore and nurture connection. Thus a working community is constructed in which members feel enriched.

Douglas Hall (1996) states, "The new career contract is not a pact with the organization; it is an agreement with one's self and one's work" (p. 10). The "agreement" insists on balance and stipulates that one cannot work in a political, power-driven, manipulating, and cynical working environment and expect to go home with a healthy attitude. Wherever they are in the circle, members are insisting on opportunities to have more ownership of their work and their workplace community. The motivation to invest themselves in such ownership requires that their work include the ingredients of (1) competence, (2) challenge, (3) empowerment, and (4) significance nurtured by interaction across the workplace circle (see Figure 1).

Competence

Competence is tied to member capabilities. Core competencies dictate whether members can do the work for which they are accountable. Clay Carr (1993) states that there are five forms of competence: job competence, interpersonal and communica-

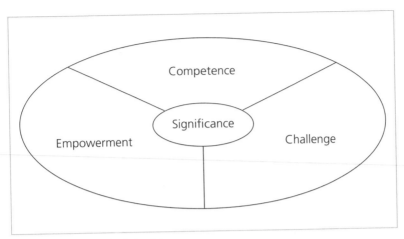

FIGURE 1   Model of Significance

tion competence, background competence (skills when hired), contextual or organizational competence (knowing the company), and self-management competence, which is "a necessary condition for all the rest" of the competences. Mastery of core competences is important to the member's ability to be a top performer in the organization. One weak link creates the potential for failure in all competences, jeopardizing the success of the individual and potentially of the organizational community. For example, one leader-member who knew his job and the work of his people well (technical knowledge) was also knowledgeable in organizational competence and was an informal leader, indicating that his interpersonal and communication skills were acceptable. Yet he was abusive of his co-members through gossip and rumors. His self-management competence was faulty. Ultimately, the fallacy was no longer accepted, even by a most tolerant manager; he was moved to a lesser position where his talents and skills were lost to the company and himself.

A key element of mastering work is the opportunity to *become* competent. Assigning people an accountability they cannot possibly do well without providing an opportunity to learn and improve creates stress, fear, insecurity, and the probability of low performance or failure.

Competent members become more credible, more productive, more involved, and more important to the organizational community and its customers. The four knowledge-based ingredients essential to top performance by the individual member are business understanding, technical understanding, interpersonal skills, and intellectual skills.

Business Understanding

In order for a member to participate knowledgeably, he or she must know *who, how, what, why,* and *where* information about the company.

Knowing *who* is the best source of information, materials, and resources makes a difference. Such resource people are often behind-the-scenes, unnoticed, and unheralded co-members. These valued resource persons also provide feedback and accountability as well as ideas. Such willingness to *work with* others in an atmosphere of informality creates opportunities for productive partnerships that are strengthened over time. Trust is basic to healthy, productive, connected human relationships. It grows when a partnership is consistently able to work well for both partners in times of quiet or of chaos. The reciprocal trusting relationship also allows for imperfection and error—humanness is allowed, even encouraged. Whether this valued resource is a hidden treasure or an out-front leader-member, believing that he or she is mindful of the member's well-being creates a connection that stimulates reciprocity of support, sponsorship, and concern for achievement.

The *how* includes an understanding of the organization's processes, culture, customers, structure, financial position, and level of success in its specific industry. Members desire to understand how to best do their work and how their work responsibilities affect opportunities for the organization to grow and make a profit. Feelings of significance can be a direct result of members' understanding how their role fits into the scheme of things and why they need to do their job well.

The *what* includes understanding the vision, mission, and strategies of the company. The members seek to also understand that what they hear is not just rhetoric to impress customers; they want to see that leaders and members believe in the ads and promotionals. Credibility and trust are not automatic; they are earned.

At a large meeting, a prominent CEO talked about all the great things that were happening at his organization—paradigms were changing, quality was improving dramatically, empowerment was being "pushed down into the organization," and employees were happy. An attendee sitting next to me was fidgeting, breathing deeply, and rolling his eyes. When I finally asked what was going on, he said, "I can hardly sit here and listen to this hogwash. I live near his headquarters and all I hear from friends and relatives— one is even a vice president—is that working for [that company] is bad. A good many of them are actively looking for other jobs. Does he really believe everything he is saying?" Apparently that CEO wasn't fully aware of what was happening in his organization. Perhaps communication of the bad things stopped at the VP level. The CEO was not getting the "what" in the organization—or what he did hear was colored, even untrue for the organizational members he appeared not to relate to.

The *why* makes it possible for members to know what is going on and how they can participate in resolving the issues and problems the organization is facing. Consistently receiving information prepares members for outcomes that are positive or negative. Hearing the good things about the organization increases member's pride in being part of the organizational community and gives them something to be positive about with their customers, friends, and families.

Hearing the good things also helps members survive the bad news when it inevitably comes. The bad news encourages members at all levels to be alert to improvements that can create innovative opportunities for them and for their communities. If members do not know the "why," they are surprised when bad news comes and become skeptical of good news.

At a party, a driver for a delivery organization heard a friend talk about something really good that was happening at his organization that would require a big delivery services contract, which was currently out for bid. The driver knew the whys of his own organization and that it needed to grow to survive. He went to his sales rep the next day to alert the rep about the opportunity. The organization had not been invited to bid, but the salesperson called on the friend's organization that day to request information and a chance to bid. He wrote and delivered a proposal the next day (the last day of proposal acceptance), and won and finalized the contract within a week. The driver was responsible for that contract, which increased the bottom line and "grew" the small organization into a contender in delivery services in its city. By knowing "why" (his organization needed to grow), the driver was alert to a possible contract opportunity for his company—and acted on it.

The *where* involves members knowing where they can make a significant contribution to their organization. To do so, they regularly ask themselves, Where are my talents most needed, and am I using my abilities in this area? Where do I fit in this organization? Members are not always hired, promoted, or assigned responsibilities that are best fitted to their talents or to the needs of the community as a whole. If members are in a misfit situation, their contributions may be limited, stonewalled, or discounted. Being alert to where the best niche is, preparing for it, and going for it can increase members' ability to feel significant in their jobs.

Being at the right place to contribute and feel comfortable is key to an individual member's achievement and positive outlook. Learning early on that this organization is not a good fit allows members to be realistic about expectations if they stay—or to leave before their investment in the organization (and the organization's investment in them) is too high.

Technical Understanding

It is important for members to have the specific knowledge and skills required to perform in their own area of responsibility as well as a general knowledge of the technical needs of the organization as a whole. When members discuss the organization with customers, their own credibility and the organization's can be harmed if they give erroneous information or make claims that are not reasonable or achievable. If members are responsible for learning, at a minimum, an overview of the technical areas of the organization, they will be able to say, "I don't know, but I will find out for you and let you know"—and then follow through immediately.

Interpersonal Skills

In a survey regarding employee traits preferred by employers *Communication Briefings*™ (1991) found that 84 percent of the employers that responded favored interpersonal skills (including good manners and the ability to get along well with others); 79 percent wanted members who could write well; 68 percent were looking for good speaking abilities; and 40 percent were looking at potential members' educational backgrounds and work experiences. It appears that education and work skills can be learned—but organizations do not have time to mold a new member's interpersonal skills, if indeed they can be taught. Employers are looking for relational members who can get the job done, participate in an environment of teamwork and cooperation, and have a head start by knowing how to work with others.

Interpersonal skills in dealing with co-members and customers are often based on the individual's relational perspective. The question is, is the member focused on the "first person" (self) or on the "third person" (others)?

The first-person perspective is I-me-us-we. Focusing on "me" may limit the member's ability to establish relationships and be empathetic, flexible, or synergistic. Being me-oriented may also prevent acceptance and "fit" in today's new business environment. Me-oriented people may view differences as threats to "my viewpoint"; they see differences as fact based; they are uncompassionate and inflexible. They find competition comfortable, cooperation not as comfortable.

Being in a team environment may be difficult from a first-person perspective. It takes too much time and requires listening to the input of others. Helping others succeed is not "my" first priority. The me-oriented person likes quick results and short-term, focused decisions, which may or may not be to the best benefit of the organization. It may not occur to me-firsters to stop and look for the impact on the company. Instead, they want to be sure the outcome will benefit "me" or "mine" (that is, they want benefits for their department; they want to keep members in their good graces).

The third-person perspective is focused toward others—he-she-him-her-they-them—outside of "self." Members with a third-person perspective have the ability (and orientation) to appreciate the contributions of others, are flexible enough to allow others to change or bring balance to their own viewpoints, and as a result are open to possibilities. The third-person perspective is relationally based; emotions are okay, and compassion is a part of the outlook. Third-person people believe you get back what you give out. They welcome opportunities to work with others on teams and in groups, and they look at the needs of others. They base their own success on meeting the needs of both their organization and those around them. Their decisions are long-term focused, and co-member consequences are thought through. First-person–oriented co-members may view the third-person perspective as soft. But they need to remember that it is out of our relationships and our interpersonal perspective that we develop meaning, rationalities, a sense of value, moral interest, motivation, and so on (McNamee & Gergen, in press). Our workplace relationships expand our appreciation or nonappreciation of our workplace community.

An organization may have a preferred interpersonal perspective, identifiable by the way it views member success. Who gets promoted and who gets ignored? Whose ideas are listened to and whose ideas are discounted? Does the organization make decisions without considering the consequences to the members involved? Who is included in decision-making processes? Are "less-than" and "more-than" status relationships subtly enforced? Are only suggestions from "appropriate" members considered valid? Who is empowered? Are messengers who share concerns perceived as being out of step, as not being team members? What is the level of resistance to change by organizational members? Is failure punished by the kiss of career death and is forgiveness impossible? Observe what is happening and take the pulse of the organization around you. We become what we tolerate.

Intellectual Skills

A collective membership with good intellectual skills is vital to the success of the organization. Intellectual skills are knowledge based and are often a training issue. Hiring a member who has high potential but lacks work skills is feasible when the organization is willing to invest in education and training of the membership. A member who has learned to solve problems, manage conflict, run a computer, communicate appropriately, and then apply those skills in work (and life) responsibilities is a value-added member, who grows every time a skill is applied. (What will happen in organizations that are firing much of their valuable intellectual asset base and keeping the status-quo-oriented members? Hiring [or retaining] a member with low growth potential is deadly for organizations.)

Providing opportunities for growth at all levels of the organization enhances all members' feelings of pride and connection to the organization. Training of the overall membership in stress, change, and time management is beneficial and demonstrates respect for members' abilities to contribute to the betterment of the organization. Investing in organizational members is a bottom-lines issue.

For example, one forward-looking organization provided workshops (for nonfinancial members at all levels) on how to read the corporate financial materials. The degree of interest in the workshops was a shock to the leaders of the organization. But for the members and shareholders, there was a big incentive to learn how to decipher those numbers instead of waiting for someone else to tell them what the numbers said, and it increased trust in information from the financial sector in the organization.

Challenge

Challenge addresses feelings of self-worth and faith that co-members believe in each other's potential to perform and add value. Value-added members are challenged to a point where they must stretch to achieve yet they do not feel that their goals are unattainable. They also challenge others by asking good questions and continually being aware. Challenge builds self-worth and alleviates paralysis caused by routinization. Boredom is a horrible thing to face every day, all day. The amount of energy a person puts into work reveals how challenged that person feels by the job.

Two aspects of challenge may affect how members feel about their jobs: *being challenged (internal)* and *challenging others (external)*. Both are connected to the willingness and ability to perform.

Being Challenged

Being challenged at work connects to the member's level of motivation and to a willingness to be highly responsible in work accountabilities. Thus internal feelings of being highly challenged may directly affect how members perform on the job.

Feeling challenged may come from within or may be activated by others. An actively contributing member has a natural inclination to perform accountabilities well and often willingly invests extra effort to do so. The underchallenged and nonchallenging member may be performing below expected levels, have no sense of urgency for work, and/or be hypercritical or negative about co-members and the organization.

Being Challenged to Change

When a member is willing to challenge his or her own performance, or is being challenged by others to do so, it is important to acknowledge that change can be painful but that positive change can bring unforeseen personal growth and enrichment. Commitment to the process of change by the member and the coach/sponsor is key to success.

For successful performance change to happen, members must first see a *need* for change. They may feel internal discomfort, which indicates the need for change, or the discomfort may be caused by the input of others such as leader-members or co-members.

Once accepted as a valid goal, successful performance change is accomplished more easily with the commitment of support from others. To do it alone usually means failure. Members can only sustain commitment with the encouragement and constructive feedback of respected others. Thus sponsorship (discussed further in Chapter Eight) of a respected leader is a key factor in the attainment of long-term change. In an organization where working *with* is the way of working, member support in dealing with personal change is possible.

Of course, having a reasonable goal is important. The self-set or agreed-to performance goals to be achieved in a reasonable length of time can provide a light at the end of the tunnel. Setting personal goals that contribute to the overall goals of the individual's department and organization often influence the member toward change.

The person's willingness to invest his or her time and energy is crucial. Individual determination is sustained by a need to change and anticipation of potential benefits from that change.

The challenge remains with the member to effect successful change. Vogt and Murrell (1990) suggest that, "the human species is capable of modifying its behavior . . . whenever survival demands it" (p. 8). Where there is a need for new performance levels in our work or with our co-members, we are capable of change and improvement. It is having the *desire* to make the choice to reconstruct ourselves or our work skills that will ultimately make the difference.

Asking Intentional Questions

Examining personal intentions toward work and assumptions of the organization's perspective may increase members' willingness to challenge their own performance. People have economic and relational reasons for staying on the job. Certain questions reveal an individual's intentions to perform (see Chart 7). How one answers the questions and what actions one takes as a result may influence decisions about staying on the job and whether there can be a better personal future on the job. The questions cover two areas: self and organization.

Giving honest, forthright answers to these questions can provide a realistic picture of one's ability to change and to create a positive future in the organization. Entitled employees will struggle with these questions and may see themselves as performing "acceptably." Of course, their answers to the question "Do I have reasonable expectations of my organization?" may be different from those of the earning member, as will be the answers to the question about "reasonable expectations of my

CHART 7   Intentional Questions

Self

- What are my strengths, and am I using them in my work?
- Do I enjoy what I am doing?
- Am I competent to do my work?
- What amount of responsibility am I willing to take in doing my work?
- Am I willing to take responsibility for my own employability in the future?
- Do I look for worst case scenarios or seek the viewpoint of opportunities?
- Do I have reasonable expectations of my organization?

Organization

- Does the organization actively support me as an individual?
- Do the members understand the organizational purpose and the customers being served?
- Does the organization have reasonable expectations of my performance?
- Are organizational co-members willing to work collaboratively to achieve the goals of the organization?
- Is the organization open to different viewpoints and diverse members?
- Is the organization actively blurring the lines so members can work effectively across levels?
- Does the organization reward successful collaborative partnering?

performance." The hope is that the discomfort members experience when approached about personal change will motivate them to realistically examine their responses and create in them a genuine desire to challenge their own performance.

Challenging Others

The second challenge is *challenging others*—the members' direct involvement in questioning, learning from, and informing. Kouzes and Posner (1993) tell us, "The antidote to rigidity is challenge" (p. 265). They designate challenge as a leader role, but all members of the organization have a role in addressing rigidity issues in the organization. Successfully challenging others (1) starts with our own awareness or concern and is performed to raise the awareness or concern of others, (2) is a tool for organizational improvement at every level of the organization, and (3) must be done in the right way.

Challenging others is externally focused and involves the consultative role of the member. Challenging raises the awareness of others through questioning, clarifying, providing information openly, addressing issues of concern to the appropriate person, and choosing active, positive involvement in the success and growth of the organization. Challenging promotes awareness of concerns and opportunities. In an organization in which listening to *all* members is a priority, challenging is accepted, encouraged, and welcomed. When members participate in positive ways in the process of identifying and sharing best practices, each participant learns from others. Challenging helps members *know that* and *know how. Knowing that* is about seeing, observing, and learning; *knowing how* is about putting that knowledge in action and shaping it for others to understand in order to allow for new, effective ways of working (Gergen, 1991).

Challenging in the right way is a higher level of involvement and membership, is appropriate and constructive, and stimulates opportunities for further involvement. Challenging appropriately encourages organizational recognition of the value of all members and honors the significance of the individual in the organization. Chart 8 illustrates the concept.

Active, positive challenging includes questioning, informing, and supporting activities that are performed with the intention of contributing to the welfare of the individual or the organization. The challenging member is an "earning" member who understands the importance of every member's expertise and collaborative efforts. Appropriate challenging means (1) positive, trusting relations can exist; (2) open, clarifying communication is expected; (3) empowerment is encouraged at all levels; (4) every member can have influence; and (5) members are seen as capable, knowledgeable, and significant to the success of the organization. Then "we are the organization" can become an actuality.

CHART 8	Actions of Challenging	
	Positive (Constructive)	Negative (Destructive)
Active	*Earning* Asking, input, influence, examining, trusting	*Entitlement* Campaigning, complaining, covertness, competition
Passive	*Nonresponse* Acceptance, patience, compliance	*Disconnect Response* Cynicism and negativity, psychologically walking away, leaving

Note: "Earning" and "Entitlement" are designations made by Judith M. Bardwick (1991), in *Danger in the Comfort Zone,* regarding a member's attitudes of contribution or entitlement (belief that something is deserved based on past performance or circumstances) on the job.

The passive, positive activity of challenging is a nonresponse or at the most a feigned response of support. The passive, positive activity (or nonactivity) (1) can reflect acceptance or patience; (2) may be seen as appropriate in organizations in which nonresponse is "the right way of being"; (3) is potentially a wait-and-see stance for the unconvinced, wary, or fearful; (4) has little impact on the discussion or the situation; (5) may make the person appear "loyal" in the entitled organization. Passive, positive members are quiet and attempt to make the appropriate gestures of approval or disapproval. They watch their supervisor and co-workers to see how they should respond.

The negative, active challenging activity is destructive and sabotaging and includes actions of campaigning, complaining, covertness, and competition. Members may be entitled employees who (1) encourage negativity and cynicism by magnifying problems and questioning successes; (2) take no responsibility for their actions; (3) highlight negative issues from the past so they will not be forgiven or forgotten; (4) perpetuate nonconformance strategies in others through rewarding; (5) are past unsuccessful leaders; and (6) may actually care about the organization but feel helpless, hopeless, and unable to deal with the issues at hand.

The negative, passive challenging activity of the entitled employee is also destructive. These members are over the edge.

They no longer care enough to discuss what is happening; they have psychologically walked away and are potentially cynical and negative. As entitled employees, they (1) see mediocrity as the way to survive; (2) resort to doing only as the position description says; (3) ignore expanded opportunities to contribute; (4) do not respond to improvement requests; and (5) feel secure enough to continue to perform in this way. An alternative for such employees is to examine their options and disconnect from the organization—leave and take their negative, passive activities to another organization.

Challenging in the right way is seen as important to the success of individuals, projects, programs, and the organization as a whole. By expanding knowledge and sharing concerns, the organization can be flexible and adaptable in responding to or preparing for marketplace changes. Our experts are already working in our organizations at all levels, and when they see that questioning and sharing of knowledge, expertise, and concerns are genuinely sought and rewarded, they will participate—as much as they are encouraged to do so.

Empowerment

A motivator that supports feelings of hope, empowerment makes working beyond participation possible. The member who is able to take action experiences some control in solving problems, generating a hope for the future he or she sees as possible. Exercising the inner drives to take action and make decisions in areas members care about is vital to top performance, but members need to know that the organization also sees such actions of empowerment as important and appropriate.

Member empowerment is an enhancing and energizing activity. It is no longer the responsibility of our leader-members to come up with all the ideas, judge their merit, and implement them or even officially delegate to others the authority to decide or take action. As co-members and designated leaders in today's work environment, we have joint roles (wherever we are in the organization) in deciding what is considered "best practice" in getting our jobs done. Member success and the organization's success are intertwined. Both the individual and the collective organizational community must eliminate barriers to mutually accomplish and support the expansion of individual and organizational bottom lines. Leader-members do not grant empowerment; they work with members through shared authority and responsibility to make decisions and take action.

The members' willingness to perform in an empowered organizational atmosphere is a "fit" situation. The organizational climate may encourage or even insist on members working autonomously, with the power to make decisions and act on their own, yet members may actually want strong guidance and limited empowerment, preferring the old hierarchical paradigm where "doing" was what worked. Such members are actually "employees," preferring to respond rather than initiate in the workplace. They will struggle in the new work environment of involvement and deep participation.

Self-Empowerment

Self-empowerment is the base and catalyst for successful empowerment. Our attitudes and our willingness to make decisions, take risks, verbalize opinions, and take action are based on our assumption that we have the right and the responsibility to act, that one person can and does make a difference.

In other words, it is the individual who decides whether to be empowered; it is a personal choice. Customer contact members, at any level, for example, make empowered decisions to soothe an upset external customer. Customer service representatives give information that will eliminate the necessity to transfer a call—and then, if appropriate, notify the concerned stakeholders. Marketing professionals make decisions within understood parameters without asking for permission. Leader-members make decisions appropriate to the needs and responsibilities of the organization and its members that are beneficial to the organization as a whole.

Empowered Partnerships

Empowered partnerships—multiple partnering relationships of two or more members—are another form of empowerment, which cannot exist without the buy-in of the membership. In an empowered partnership, members are confident that they

---

CHART 9   Empowered Partnership

■ *Impact*
  Working together is not a waste of time. What is done matters,
  resulting in balanced consideration of bottom line decisions that
  have long-term benefits for the workplace community.

■ *Purpose*
  The partnership shares a clear and significant purpose and the desired
  outcomes target improvement, innovation, and accomplishment.

■ *Connection*
  The partnership is synergistic, creating connective opportunities for
  accomplishment that go far beyond what could have been accomplished by one.

■ *Energy*
  The members work well together, challenge each other to perform,
  and are committed to the benefits of empowered partnership. As a
  result, the energy of the group contributes to the outcomes.

---

can take action within guidelines that both partners understand,
within areas of their expertise and accountability (and potentially beyond those accountabilities), and with the added information, skills, actions, and support of the partnership involved
(see Chart 9). Of course, working in empowered partnerships
mis potentially conflicting, takes additional time and suspends
exclusive independence—all ingredients of working in isolation.

Without outcomes that are beneficial to the parties involved,
the partnership will die. To remain in partnership, the partners
must have a shared and significant purpose. If the partners feel
connected, they will be energized and committed; they will perform at a high level of responsibility and expand their abilities to
affect the bottom lines of the organization. Collectively and individually, they will feel that they are making a contribution (significance) to their own success, their group's success, and their
organization's success.

Organizational Empowerment

The third element of empowerment is *the organization*. Because
the organization is us, members collectively make empowerment succeed or fail. It is the role of the leadership team, in
partnership with the organizational members, to identify and

incorporate empowerment principles into the climate of the organization. This is an overall membership responsibility, is not limited to activities of the leader-members, and does not happen overnight.

Empowerment is in most instances a huge paradigm shift that will cause fear at all membership levels. Some leaders will not want to give up control (they see members as lazy and incompetent); some members will see it as an opportunity (finally I can do what I need to do); some will actively avoid taking responsibility (they don't pay me to make decisions); and some will wait and see how it works before they risk becoming involved.

Significance

Having significance in the sense of performance within the organization means that one's contribution is valued, important. What the member does matters, and there will be a consequence if he or she is not performing well. Members sense the degree of their worthiness in the workplace; they can tell whether or not they are a valued contributor in the organization. Significance is an outcome of all three of the other motivations for performance (competence, empowerment, and challenge). If one of the other motivators is missing, it will be difficult if not impossible for a member to achieve significance. When members are discounted and ignored, they disconnect. Conversely, when they feel connected to the organization, they enroll. Also, accomplishment of mutually held goals is more probable and less problematic when members feel significant to the accomplishment of those goals.

There is a difference in the energy members apply to performance when they sense that what they do matters. The member who is listened to and has the opportunity to have input and influence in the design of a new product or the machine that builds it is, in the process, potentially buying in to whether the product is a quality product or the machine works well. The member can then be "enrolled." Enrollment is a personal choice—an act of belief that what one does is worthwhile (significant). Co-members or the organization cannot enroll a member in the work he or she performs or in the organization. The organization can make it possible for the member to enroll by providing the opportunity for the member to be *willing* to enroll. The responsibility rests with the collective organization to create and nurture an environment and culture where members are willing to assume responsibility for what they say and what they can potentially or actually do (Cheney & Carroll, 1997). Although enrollment is a personal act, the organization makes enrollment and feelings of significance possible.

In order to understand how they are valued in their organization, members seek a comfort level of significance. Feelings of significance signal to members that their work is important to the overall organizational community. Unconsciously, members set boundaries that tell them whether or not they are significant to the performance of their group and organization.

Levels of logic or comparison points provide a sense of being or not being valued in one's organization; they are self-set and different for each person. In today's working arena, there is a new understanding that each member must contribute to the amount he or she earns—each member's job must matter. When members sense no value or insignificance, they are afraid of losing their job. Levels of logic include identity, continuity, equilibrium, and feelings of fairness.

Identity

Significance is triggered by *identity*, a sense of belonging to or linking with the organization. As noted previously, identity is seeing where we fit in the organization, understanding our importance to the achievement of the goals of the organization, knowing that we make a difference and that if we are not there it matters. A strong identity in the organizational picture nurtures feelings of significance and justifies "going the extra mile." When feelings of identity are in place, people feel safe, which nurtures feelings of significance even in the face of failure.

Continuity

Another measure of significance is the assumption of *continuity*. Every workday, situations arise that either support or undermine the members' feelings of continuity, certainty, and security. Karl

Weick (1995) states, "Sensemaking involves taking whatever is clearer, whether it be belief or action, and linking it with that which is less clear" (p. 135). Members perceive incidences of disempowerment, distrust, or noncompetence as contradictions. They begin to doubt their previously held sense of the continuity of acceptance and wonder if they are still significant, value-added people in the organization. Such incidents result in disconnections and produce anxiety. The member suddenly feels that the circle has gotten smaller; it no longer stretches to include him or her. His or her sense of continuity is interrupted. Occurrences of uncertainty are sensed as temporary contradictions of certainty. Significance allows members to understand that lines of contradiction are "learning events,"not threats to continuity.

Equilibrium

Significance includes an understanding that *equilibrium* is a flow of success *and* failure that affects the member's willingness to move beyond participation to top performance and contribution. Deep participation creates swings between success and failure; learning takes place during those swings. When members are feeling unsafe, significance is threatened but the members learn the most. If leaders convince members that this territory is an acceptable byproduct of working beyond participation, members will continue to feel significant even in times of disequilibrium.

Feelings of Fairness

Perceptions of *fairness or unfairness* affect the member's sense of significance. Each person has expectations of how members of the organizational community should be treated and what is fair or unfair. Organizations are imperfect because they are made up of humans with human frailties. Unfortunately, the unforgiving attitudes of many members demand an impossible level of perfection. The degree to which members acknowledge imperfection and challenge the organization (in the right way) to deal fairly and appropriately with members—while practicing forgiveness—is directly connected to their sense of significance.

Interaction

Interaction facilitates significance. In Western culture, words count. Visitors from other countries comment on the openness, curiosity, and straightforwardness of Americans, which sometimes makes them uncomfortable. For Westerners, being noninteractive makes other Westerners suspicious and destroys the opportunity for an open and informal exchange.

For all members, successful interaction is crucial. It paves the road to acceptance and achievement. A member cannot affect the significance of self or others unless he or she is seen as competent (or can achieve competence). The member cannot be empowered or offer empowerment without willingly interacting with others. Nor can the member be challenged or challenge others without participating in ongoing, successful interaction.

Summary

When members cannot reach a comfort level of the motivational factors of competence (capability), empowerment (hope), challenge (self-worth), and significance (importance), they are unlikely to enroll or re-enroll in an organization. There is no energy; mediocre performance prevails; and disconnection fosters fear and wariness. When the organizational community holds to the concepts of the Membership Organization while striving to nurture these motivational factors, members will look back and see the changes that built on one another, ultimately increasing the three bottom lines of the organization (discussed in Chapter Four) and increasing the individual member's realization of significance to the achievement of organizational success.

4

When people have been left out of decisions, they often feel powerless and unneeded. They become dependent on others, anxious about their value to the organization, cynical in their dealings, and understandably resistant to well-intentioned efforts to "empower" people.

Kathleen D. Ryan and
Daniel K. Oestriech,
Driving Fear Out of the Workplace

Decisioning

> The identification of potential long-term outcomes for the organization, as well as for the internal and external customers and the community, are central to the decisioning process.

In the years when having an MBA from one of the big schools mattered, the only bottom line was the financial one. Fresh-faced MBAs were hired to strategize and lay out the path for the organization for five or ten years. Strategic planning produced The Plan—a set of documents that guided organizational, departmental, and personal goal setting. Afterward, it was relegated to a dark drawer never to be seen again— until evaluation time rolled around. Two weeks prior to performance reviews, people scrambled to find their dusty copy of The Plan in order to throw together explanations as to why their performance and outcomes did not go according to The Plan.

Times have changed. Now decision making is "decisioning," an ongoing process that can be done on your feet and acted on as needed. No longer is there time for endless strategy meetings. All members—wherever they are inside the organizational circle—are responsible for decisioning to meet the goals of the organization.

Although vision, goals, and planning remain vital to the success of the organization, flexibility and adaptability are the guiding plan. What worked yesterday may not work today and certainly won't work tomorrow. In the current organizational community environment, with or without the guidance of an MBA, the new planning and decisioning process has to include *everyone* inside the organizational circle—and must be based on balanced consideration and examination of the three bottom lines.

Decision Making/Decisioning

Researchers tell us that the success of decision making depends primarily on decision quality, decision acceptance, and the amount of time needed to make the decision. Of course, selecting the decision process depends on the overall organizational climate, and the decision quality will depend on having the right people involved in that process. How leader-members view members' abilities and to what degree members are routinely involved in decisioning will also influence the process to be used. When leader-members routinely demonstrate collaborative decisioning processes, this affects member perceptions of partnership and membership in their organizations. In the past, the primary types of decision procedures were

- *Autocratic.* The leader makes a decision alone without input from individuals or group members and then shares and "sells" the decision.
- *Consultative.* The leader shares the problem with the individual or group and asks for input but makes the decision autonomously.
- *Group Decisioning.* The leader discusses the issue with the individual or group and makes a decision that is mutually acceptable (at least with the majority of the group). The leader participates but attempts no influence over the outcome (Yukl, 1990).

In the Membership Organization, the decisioning process is performed in an atmosphere of empowerment, co-membership, and participation. Turf issues are resolved and the group looks

CHART 10 Decision Making vs. Decisioning	
Decision Making (Old Paradigm)	
Autocratic:	Leader tells
Consultation:	Leader asks group, decides alone
Group Decision:	Leader discusses, group decides
Decisioning (New Paradigm)	
Membership:	Expert(s) facilitate; group decides

for ways to address the issues faced by all participants, both individually and collectively. The group mutually decides in a framework of deep participation. Input and feedback appropriately challenge quick, conventional decision processes. The facilitator of the group is the expert-member who contributes information as needed in the area of the decision, whatever his or her member location in the workplace circle. Issues are discussed, and a mutually acceptable decision is made (or not made). Chart 10 illustrates the difference between decision making and decisioning.

But decisioning is not always a group process. Top performance requires that decisioning expertise be moved to the people who know the problems and have the most knowledge on how to deal with them, whoever they may be. To make this possible, leader-members must learn to trust the co-members at the outer edges of the circle to make accurate, informed decisions. When members are educated and trained appropriately and given the go-ahead to do what needs to be done, they can perform far beyond the usual; top performance *can* result from learning and experiencing. In some cases, however, members attend training, learn new skills and processes, and get enthusiastic about applying their new skills, only to be disempowered by leaders who "get in the way." The leader just can't let go. He or she is always checking, rechecking, and changing the member's decisions. The member still is not in the decisioning loop. In other cases, the member really doesn't want to make decisions. This member goes off to the training session, half-heartedly listens, and then upon returning throws up his or her hands in feigned frustration when decisioning opportunities occur. In this case, it is not as important for the member to take training as it is for training to "take" with the member.

Members notice what the decision routines are in their group or organization and interpret what they see. An attitude of "NETMA" (nobody ever tells me anything) tends to develop from routine, closed, nonparticipative decision processes of the group or organization. However, creating open channels that empower members throughout the circle passes the responsibility to get information and participate in decisioning to everyone in the organizational community, blurring even more the lines of status and control.

In the new mind-set of decisioning, participation means that input and empowerment become a community norm. Group involvement in decisioning symbolizes deep participation, solidifying the members' level of responsibility for the success, failure, or stagnation of the organization.

Bottom Lines

Ultimately the actions, attitudes, and decisions of the individual and the collective organizational membership affect the organizational bottom lines—financial, social, and human. These three bottom lines are inseparable, interlinked, and exponential. We all understand that without a financial foundation, an organization could not employ members. Interdependence of the three shows that what detracts from the human bottom line eventually detracts from the financial and social bottom lines of the organization as well. Also, what detracts from the social bottom line affects the positioning or image of the company, and eventually the financial and human bottom lines suffer. Albrecht (1979, p. 311) adds, "Without the human payoff in money, job satisfaction, personal fulfillment, respect for human values and human rights, and opportunities for individual growth, the economic bottom line becomes harder and harder to maintain. The price for inhuman use of human beings must be paid sooner or later, and I believe *it is always paid in actual dollars and cents.*" (Albrecht's italics.)

In the past, organizational representatives focused decision making only on the financial bottom line, using financial statistics to rationalize and justify previous decisions made out of a linear "certainty" that did not consider the human and social bottom lines. Presenting the financial answer as correct eliminated all motivation to examine the social and human elements of the issue in question. Human and social concerns were examined only to figure out how to justify the expected outcome, or they were ignored.

Global Perspective

A more global consideration process, which, of course, may ultimately result in favoring one of the bottom lines, provides for open discussion of outcomes. The member who balances social, human, and financial decisioning is using common sense. He or she is more flexible, directly involved, and often innovative, and has a tendency to take action where needed, within the boundaries of all three bottom-line considerations. The financial bottom-line–oriented person, not interested in seeing the social and human bottom lines, makes decisions that are impersonal, detached, fact based; the social and human considerations are inconsequential and problem producing. In this atmosphere, membership principles and perspectives cannot flourish. Donald Wolfe (1988) says, "Whenever people say, 'The bottom line is . . .' you can be sure they want to cut off consideration of competing possibilities" (p. 145) and, [they have] "little need for knowledge of the people whose lives are altered by [decisions they make]" (p. 148).

Moving to a more global perspective means changing what an organization's members believe the organization values (Schneider, Brief, & Guzzo, 1996). It takes concerted effort and consistency on the part of leader-members to present, validate, emphasize, and follow through with the importance and benefits of decisioning made through examination of all three bottom lines.

When deciding members believe that fat bottom lines justify sacrificing people and society, that survival of the fittest means being an anorexic organization—lean and mean to the detriment of the survivors—the message is loud and clear. Members understand the focus of the leadership. As one member of a West Coast company said, "Our core value is money and everyone knows it." For the financially flush organization, when a problem occurs, throw money at it. When there is an image problem, send out the PR people to polish it up—and throw money at it. But don't change the way things are really being done. For the financially adequate organization, increase the financial bottom line by downsizing—"in order to ensure the future." For the financially struggling organization, lay off those with valuable expertise and loyalty—really cripple the company; the desire for quick-fix financial stability results in a sacrificed future.

The Human Bottom Line

In the past, leaders made rational, detached, numbers-based decisions potentially at the expense of the internal members and external customers of the organizational community. "Human capital" decisions weren't hard to make. Members were expendable: No problem—others could replace them. Long-term, dedicated service received little if any consideration when numbers dipped. For example, organizations sometimes made conscious decisions to release members with long service records when high payouts were indicated at a later time.

Then things changed. Jobs shifted to high tech, requiring highly skilled members, in whom organizations invested large amounts of money for training. Competition for trained members increased. New members throughout the circle, from inside to the edge, began to require costly training and extensive investment in maintenance of their skills. In these organizations, home-grown experts have come to mean something to the organizational community. Clearly the human bottom line has become critical to success. For this reason, long-term human resource forecasting uses a combination of quantitative method and subjective judgment and must include looking at all three bottom lines in order to make beneficial long-term decisions.

Financial Affect

The human bottom line, complicated as it is, makes a significant difference in the financial bottom line. Patricia McLagan and

Christo Nel (1995) in *The Age of Participation* (a must read for membership organization leaders) states that "research [described in the book] conducted since the mid-1980s strongly suggests that participation is worth the price. Companies that constantly and broadly involve their people in what used to be managerial work are more productive and financially successful than companies that do not."

Organizational leaders are now waking up to the complexity of the workplace. They have recognized for years that systems are complicated; they are just now awakening to the fact that organizations are human by nature. As human organizations, they are dependent on *people* to address issues relating to the financial bottom line. And, ultimately, as noted by Deal and Jenkins (1994), "[Human organizations] are delightfully surprising and deceptive. Compliance does not always follow command. Change does not always make things much different. Taking another obvious jump, a person's contribution is not always determined by [his or her] placement in the formal pecking order" (p. 24). People care about what organization they work for, what it does, and how it is perceived in the external community. When they identify with the mission and purpose of their organization, they work with dedication and determination.

Fairness and Unfairness

A human bottom line issue that can indirectly affect the financial well-being of the organization is the perception of fair treatment in the everyday occurrences in the workplace. An expectation of perfection in the workplace affects members' willingness to forgive and forget. Members routinely see their leaders as representatives of the organization; when the organizational representative is not perfect (does something unforgivable) and the member feels unable to seek justice, repetition of unfair treatment may bring cynicism. Research has shown that previously high-performing members who feel they have been treated unfairly are potentially the most cynical members in the workplace (Wanous, Reichers, & Austin, 1994).

Perceptions of fairness or unfairness (as discussed in Chapter Three) are catching; they move across the organizational circle, eventually affecting the climate of the organizational community and its ability to be a top performer. For this reason, the best interests of the member should be of concern to everyone in the organization. Perceptions of fairness and unfairness are based on the following assumptions:

Members must be able to participate in decisions. Deep participation requires that members have the power to influence decisions pertaining to their work and their welfare. Studies have demonstrated that doing repetitive work, without a sense of control over activities, increases a member's feeling of alienation. Influencing opportunities create a sense of inclusion and connection to the purpose of the organization, making top performance possible for the individual and the group being influenced.

Members are assumed to be capable of free and constructive deliberation. Inclusiveness provides opportunities for clarification of policies and procedures that are perceived as unfair. There must be a commitment to viewing members as autonomous agents who can successfully challenge (question) the system, a significant implication for the organizational community. When a person is recognized as being productive, and performs decisioning on his or her own, that person has a sense of personal responsibility. Open, productive, inclusive decisioning processes connect the membership to the immediate and overall goals of the organization.

When individual members believe themselves to be powerful (as opposed to powerless), it enhances their self-respect and self-worth. Psychologists contend that dignity is related to signals received in the workplace that members are worthwhile people (McCall, 1995). Instances of perceived fairness or unfairness affect their feelings of hope, capability, and worthiness, and are extensions of dignity (Zolno, 1996). Feelings of worthiness and perceptions of performance excellence contribute to members' willingness to exert influence, which in turn makes them feel that respect is deserved. Being treated with dignity thus creates dignity.

The Social Bottom Line

Organizations are now facing greater scrutiny from community as well as from membership, and justifiably so. Organizational leaders' understandings of social issues are often encumbered by their "entitled" attitudes—"after all we've done for this community!"—which displays insensitivity to many issues. Addressing deficiencies in the organization's public responsibility and facing criticism of product/service integrity and good citizenship require an attitude change. Organizations need to adopt new beliefs and values regarding social responsibility.

The healthy social bottom line of the organization requires the leader-members to believe that the organization has certain social responsibilities to the surrounding community in order for both to survive. This social awareness and the resulting gestures will also influence beliefs and activities of the organization's internal members regarding many social issues.

Environmentalism

The activism of the 1960s and 1970s demanded that the business community assume a role in society's environmental realities and limitations. Laws were designed, the media became a self-proclaimed watchdog, and changing mind-sets of organizational members increased awareness and brought demands for more than mere compliance with the law. Commitment of top managers, industry-specific codes of ethics, and involvement of the members generated new environmental management systems and programs with quantifiable goals and clear implementation plans. New guidelines were established by the corporations themselves for minimizing risk and sustaining an environmental vision. Such visions embraced unique characteristics of an individual organization's environment and influenced the beliefs and values of the members regarding their stewardship. New public sensibilities developed, identifying organizations as "out of compliance," "in compliance," or "environmentally friendly." As a result of these changes, it is no longer financially feasible for an organization to be inattentive to the impact it has on its external environment.

Societal Needs

Early in the 1990s, the public began to demand that the business community accept more responsibility for human suffering. Decreases in government services to the poor and the disadvantaged increased needs for localized social services. Downsizing of faltering organizations released formerly secure members into the ranks of the unemployed. For many, jobs were not readily available. The strains on already stretched funding sent social agencies to the business community for help.

Philanthropy

When organizations participate in the social welfare of their external communities, their actions validate and acknowledge the nonprofit organization they are helping. For this reason, businesses have power to influence the social context in which they operate. Businesses and the public now recognize that power and the need for organizations to be involved in the spheres in which they do business and earn profits.

The implication is that caring organizations want to participate in philanthropic initiatives not just for the sake of the positive image they create but also for the sake of those who enable the corporation to earn profits—its members. Ten years ago, in a conversation with James Gregory Lord of Philanthropic Quest International, Dr. Gordon Moore, co-founder of Intel, said that it was not the market share or the financial bottom line that caused him and Intel to be interested in the environment. "It's because our employees want it. They want us to be a green company."

The arena of business is still focused on "enlightened self-interest," the banner of corporate philanthropy for many decades. But there is a change in what constitutes self-interest. When the Japanese set up manufacturing plants in the United States, they were told by their American counterparts, "If you want to do business here, you've got to jump into philanthropy." And they responded with, "Show me. What good will it do us?" That seemed to usher in a time when U.S. businesses began to move from undifferentiated generosity and altruism ("If this is good for the community, it's good for us")to a more focused "How does this fit with our business strategy?" approach. For many reasons, the corporation now seeks to be more accountable to the stockholder, able to defend its philanthropic decisions.

These days, the justification for spending extraordinary sums on corporate philanthropy is in making the environment in which the corporation operates more conducive to fulfilling the corporation's objectives. For this reason, participation in social philanthropy is always carefully planned. Responsibility lies with the organizational decisioner to make wise and educated decisions regarding social support and involvement.

Investment in philanthropy (1) requires that the investigator be committed to the consideration, (2) demands that there be a reason for the investment, and (3) insists that the investment make a difference. Without these ingredients, the act of philanthropy is meaningless, outside the scope of identified philanthropic goals, and possibly ill advised. Just handing out money opens the door to incompetent use of the investment, results in inconsistent benefits of philanthropic gestures, and invites concern on the part of organizational members and stockholders.

Such handouts also lessen the opportunity of the philanthropist organization (or individual) to "experience" philanthropy. When an organization fails to establish connections to the nonprofit's purpose, the members of the organization fail to experience the value of contributing to the welfare of an external local, national, or global social community.

Lord asks, "Is a particular corporation an isolated island of profit, or is it a participant in or member of its industry, or of the local community, or of its nation, or of the world? And what happens when you are a member of a corporation that takes seriously its membership in the family of humanity and humanity's home? How large is your organization's world? And just what does the decision of the corporation to be a community citizen or a global citizen mean to the person who seeks meaning through his or her affiliation—who seeks, in the words of anthropologist Dorothea Leighten, to be 'a worthwhile member of a worthwhile group?' Is this person him- or herself a citizen of the community or of the world, thanks to the connection the corporation has recognized and reinforced between itself and the greater system?"

The answer may be in the organization's definition of its "business horizon"—of what can be influenced by that organization. Or is it in recognizing the interdependency of all systems and levels of systems? In today's larger community, with ever-expanding philanthropic needs, the business horizon is something to be examined when the social responsibility of philanthropy is being considered.

The Financial Bottom Line

In the past, the financial bottom line was *the* bottom line. Hierarchical decision making was a historical reality that necessitated command and control. Decision making was slow and ponderous in the bureaucratic organization: Numbers were needed, more proof was required, and common sense was suspect. Slow responses made adaptability and agility impossible when changes in the new, chaotic business environment began to come fast and furiously. Eventually the new adaptability requirement forced gestures of pushing decisions to the outer edges of the circle—except in the area of the financial bottom line. Often cumbersome signing-off procedures remained in place. Because of past depersonalization of organizational members and tendencies to "showboat" their own performance, leaders found it hard (as many still do today) to give up that final "okay." Including those of lower status in the budgeting process was an outcome that made hierarchical leaders nervous. Surely, thought the leaders, they can't make these kinds of decisions! The members proved them wrong. As a result, the lines of status have been blurred even more.

Of course, the financial bottom line is by its nature objective. If the wrong objective decisions are made, whole organizations disappear. Thus the criticality of decisioning may focus the decisioner *only* on the financial. Novice decisioners may see focusing on this bottom line as the easiest way to accomplish admirable results. Educating such novices early in their new empowerment regarding the importance of the global decisioning outlook is significant to their performance as decisioners over time.

Looking at and deciding from a viewpoint that includes all three bottom lines is work, requires more information, may pull others into the process, and demands a more global outlook. Eventually, as organizations consistently encourage this perspective, decisioning will automatically be based on this wider viewpoint, changing the culture of decisioning in the organizational community. Top performance will include the consideration of the human and social (more subjective) aspect of decisioning alongside the number-focused (objective) aspect of the process.

The importance of the financial bottom line is not in question. It is the decisioners' propensity for making decisions *excessively* or *only* based on the financial arena that is significant to decisioning outcomes in the organization.

Characteristics of Decisioning

Organizations are composed of interdependent systems. The people in those systems have different objectives and different perspectives, agendas, and preferences that contribute to the complexities of making decisions. To make it worse, the participants are competing for scarce resources: money, influence, and outcomes. Promotion of programs, maintenance of growth, and assurance of innovation vie for funds alongside greed, status seeking, and ego enhancement within the organization. Organizations make sense of these interrelationships through the use of internal decision structures.

The internal decision structure is made up of complex rules, procedures, roles, and customs that guide its policies and actions (French, 1984). Identifying the structure with a title assumes an orderly decisioning activity made under consistent circumstances. If that were true, decisions would be made easily and with fewer outcome failures. Instead, decisioning requires the decision maker to be aware that considering all the other ramifications (social and human) may necessitate trade-offs in time, openness, involvement, and heightened complexity of an already complex process.The outcomes of more knowledge-based decisioning, easier implementation, increased reponsibility, and increased awareness make the trade-offs justifiable.

Bottom Line Mentality

To be unaware of the need for trade-offs and to not seriously consider the effects of decision outcomes on the other bottom lines is irresponsible, destroys the integrity of the decision maker and the decision, ignores the values of the organization, and fails to prevent those outcomes (Wolfe, 1988). Successful decisioning avoids the bottom line mentality, accepts the emotionality of decisioning, provides opportunities for decisioning, and recognizes that credibility, integrity, a global perspective, constructive reluctance, courage, and serendipity make superior decisioning possible.

Donald Wolfe (1988) describes the disregard of organizational values as a threat to individual and organizational integrity, calling it the "bottom line mentality." This fact-based, tunnel-visioned, limited-to-the-financial outlook does not "look for the lively possibilities in the situation" (p. 163). Wolfe describes this as a *spirit of inquiry*—looking for the hidden complexities and potentials that require creative problem solving and anticipation of unintended consequences (p. 164). He also notes that the bottom line mentality

- Involves simplistic thinking in which financial success is treated as the only value to be considered or as the value to which all others can be reduced
- Leads to disowning of other system values
- Promotes short-term, quick-fix efforts rather than genuine problem solving and progress
- Fosters adversarial relations
- Creates a sense of unreality and a tunnel vision with respect to values (p. 149)

The bottom line mentality limits the identification of innovative, productive, and long-view decisioning; excludes the input of those who consider other values; and adheres strictly to the barriers of linear thinking. The bottom line mentality flourishes on oversimplification, focusing on numbers justification of a decision, ignoring interdependencies with the human and social aspects, and eliminating consideration of all possibilities. Standardization and objectivity are the only considerations.

Emotion

Although organizational decisions may be more complex than decisions made outside of organizations, decisions are still made by people—people under pressure. As a result, decisioning is an emotional activity. The emotional response includes *anticipatory stress* and *reach-back* (Albrecht, 1979). The decisioning person who feels pressured and inadequate ("I don't have enough information!") looks at looming horrible outcomes before looking at the positive outcomes, gets sweaty palms, becomes downright mean, or avoids the decision altogether. All this is a response to anticipatory stress. Reach-back multiplies feelings of anticipatory stress and is a "period of time during which an impending event begins to influence one's behavior" (Albrecht, 1979, p. 90). For some persons, decisioning is a high hurdle.

Decisioning under the best of circumstances requires a member to make a choice. When empowerment is not real, the member becomes anxious. Anxiety limits flexibility; the member focuses on possible threats if he or she makes a wrong decision. With downsizing, members must take on additional, often unfamiliar, responsibilities; decisions made in those circumstances aggravate stress. The member performs "emotional labor"—forcing a smile, but underneath constantly fearing threats (real or unreal) due to the downsizing. To this person, effective decisioning is essential.

To perform effective decisioning requires skill in analysis and innate intuition. Henry Mintzberg (1989) identifies some of the differences between the two when used in isolation, which are summarized in Chart 11.

The obvious differences between the two decisioning styles are the concreteness of the analytical thinker, who requires more time, more knowledge, fewer emotions, more data, and one answer. The intuitive decisioner is more off-the-cuff, instinct and commonsense oriented, open to making decisions based on experience and soft data and to new ways of thinking about the issue at hand.

To combine the analytic with the intuitive is often difficult for the lone decisioner. Pressures and stress in the throes of

CHART 11 Decisioning Styles	
Analysis	Intuition
Time-consuming	Spontaneous, instinctive
Systematic	Commonsense
Nonemotional	Emotion and experience
Hard data–based	Soft data–based
Closed	Open

Note: Adapted from H. Mintzberg (1989), *Mintzberg on Management: Inside Our Strange World of Organizations.*

decisioning create feelings of concern and anxious anticipation. Decisioners who include others in the decision-making process when time is available can secure resources for marrying the analytic and the intuitive and relieve the stress of the "the -buck-stops-here" syndrome. Inclusiveness creates opportunities for "soft analysis" (a combination of the two) (Mintzberg, 1989), resulting in solutions that are workable and beneficial as well as acceptable to the participants.

Soft analysis requires what Karl Weick (1995) calls "noticing" for the best decisions to be made. To make informed decisions, decisioners need information that they may not have consciously gathered. Intuitive persons "absorb" what is going on around them—often without being aware of it. Weick says, "Noticing determines whether people consider responding to environmental events. If events are noticed, people make sense of them; and if events are not noticed, they are not available for sensemaking" (p. 52).

Weick also offers the proposition that sensemaking may be built around orderly "arguing"—the process of reducing the number of beliefs thought to be relevant. Inclusive decisioning will not always involve sensitive and low-key challenging among participants. In fact, very intense interaction can often produce decisions of relevance, as long as the process remains conducive to doing so.

Inclusive/Exclusive Decisioning

Participative organizations pay more attention than authoritarian institutions to the way in which decisions are made and who is involved (McLagan & Nel, 1996). It has long been assumed that making decisions without including those who know the most about them can lessen the value of their outcomes, indicating that the circle must be widened to include others in the decisioning process.

Organizational decisioning can be either exclusive or inclusive. *Exclusive decisioning* involves one or a few people, excluding those not included in the inner circle. *Inclusive decisioning* is a process of involvement, pulling into the process all members with vital information and concerns. Participation instead of exclusion serves as an antidote to dependence and cynicism, initiating involvement and action. The inclusiveness of decisioning partnerships in the Membership Organization is based on the consultative role of the member. Deep participation in decisioning establishes open systems in which the membership is involved or actively making decisions that matter.

Significant to membership is expanded trust in the ability of co-members to make exclusive decisions, when appropriate. Quick decisions often demand one person's expertise and understanding; calling a meeting to make such a decision is not a productive use of time for the attendees. Instead, exclusive decisioning can prove action producing and productive—and releases the empowered leadership capability of the decisioning member. The Membership Organization encourages and expects both exclusive and inclusive decisioning.

Credibility

Members who are not seen as credible are not taken seriously. Active participation over time establishes and extends the credibility factor of members. When organizations provide opportunities for exclusive and inclusive decisioning, this encourages members to stretch and learn. It also gives them the authority to influence, challenge, ask questions, request information, and invite themselves into the decisioning conversation. Credibility grows with each act of deep participation, day by day and incident by incident, demonstrating trustworthiness, excellence, and top performance.

Integrity

Enrollment and ownership by members cannot exist if organizational integrity is in question. We are a culture that values integrity; it is the modern version of honor (Maccoby, 1988). Consciously making decisions that are honest, forthright, and credible is important to those involved in the decisioning process. Members take cues from their co-members throughout the circle and especially from their leader-members as to the integrity of decisions being made. They ask themselves, who is making the decisions? What are the anticipated/real outcomes of the decisions being made? Why was this decision made? They also notice whether they are given opportunities to participate in decisions that they can influence.

The organizational leader who only reluctantly provides information for effective member influencing appears to be withholding knowledge vital to member success, thus increasing the members' doubts about the openness and honesty of the leader group. For members to actively seek influencing opportunities, they must be confident that they have timely, accurate information that helps them increase their understanding and effectiveness within the organization (Felkins, Chakiris, & Chakiris, 1993).

Leadership Styles

All of the bottom lines decisions of an organization, seemingly thought out and purposeful, are an attempt to rationalize and justify the organization's existence. Decisions must be made. The autocratic leader with a self-image as "the superior knower" (Gergen, 1991) has been replaced in many organizations with formal and informal leader-members who establish constructive, empowering partnerships within the community. The superior knower, who often has only one bottom line focus, is out of decisioning balance and is often the supreme rationalizer. The superior knower limits consideration of things he or she does not completely understand (intuitive) or does not see as central to the issue being considered. The inclusion of other perspectives is, to this person, problematic and not constructive to what he or she has already identified as the coherent answer. (Rationalizing is an attempt to shift to coherence.) Such a leader thinks that being dispassionate, rational, objective, and productive are essential when the stakes are "real" (Gergen, 1991). Eventually others lose interest in giving input and attempting to justify against the already justified. Even upon invitation, members withdraw, assuming noninclusion or that there is risk in inclusion in the decision process.

The inclusive, relational leader-member is aware that decisioning activities are risky and involve learning curves. Inclusive leader-members educate members regarding all three bottom lines and share new knowledge, thus allowing members to have broadened perspective.

Successful decisioning in the Membership Organization involves a values-based decisioning approach that is inclusive and that considers the effect of decisions on all three bottom lines. The leader-member expands the organizational circle (without sharing decisioning accountabilities, the circle cannot expand). Distributing decisioning accountabilities to those members not previously seen as credible, and active consideration of decisioning on the human and social bottom lines, support the identification of innovative alternatives, expanding the possibility of a more global decisioning perspective.

Constructive Reluctance

Reluctance is indeed constructive. The member who challenges, examines, looks for alternatives, and struggles with being convinced forces decision makers to search for the better answer, if there is one. Being "constructively reluctant" also includes the responsibility to collaborate on and connect to the decision of the group. Unconstructive resistance requires conformity to the demands of one participant who cannot be moved or cannot move others. That participant is putting up barriers to top performance for the group, and is working not at the mastery level of the continuum but rather at the level of "exclusive independence"—a component of the reliance stage of the Personal Mastery Continuum (see Chart 6, on page 47).

Courage

It takes a special kind of courage to remain reluctant or to put forward unappreciated alternatives, to remain true to one's values. In decisioning, it is courageous to have the willingness and tenacity to know what is needed and say so with passion, to know your own limitations and acknowledge them, to stand up for what you believe and lead by those beliefs while serving as an example for others.

Serendipity

Serendipity is the ability to make positive discoveries by accident. The effective member is open to sensing, noticing, seeking the different, and stepping to the edge. Here, without planned decisioning, there is "new seeing." New frameworks are designed, new opportunities arise, and innovations happen. Here is the excitement of "aha." The intuitive person prone to serendipitous decisioning must already have the facts— serendipity must fall on fertile ground. The member who is knowledgeable, curious, open to change, and searching for solutions is open to serendipitous propositions and solutions.

Summary

Making decisions whether at work or at home is never a linear process. Working with and being with others—and making decisions regarding those interdependencies—creates complexities that require new frameworks for looking at the human, social, and financial bottom lines within the context of integrity and personal and organizational values.

When "we are the organization" becomes a reality, intensified accountability and deep participation pervade the circle. Organizational members want an ideal situation; they want decisioning to consider the benefits and ramifications for furthering the internal organizational community as well as the external local and global society. All members have responsibilities to the bottom lines. Peter Drucker's (1974) message to management now applies to the entire organizational circle: "It is the task of *this* . . . generation to make the institutions of society . . . perform for society and economy; for the community; and for the individual alike" (p. 807). (Drucker's italics)

5

Humans are fashioned by their relationships. In relationships, in order to be our best, our most fulfilled, our most enabling, we must be in search of *the bold, the true, and the beautiful.* The good, the true, and the beautiful exist in each of us as well as our relationships and thus, our organizations.

Suresh Srivastva & Carla Carten,
*Academy of Management Organization
Development and Change Newsletter*

Relationship

For all members, the
"relational approach" is
basic in working with others.
It is the responsibility of
every member to establish
connecting relationships that
work and that add energy to
the individual, the group,
and the organization.

Members become isolated when they cannot connect
with co-members. For example, a detail-oriented manager,
whose micromanaging tactics drove those reporting (and not
reporting) to him to distraction, was stiff, detached, and unable
to communicate well with others. Some avoided him out of self-
defense, even scurrying to disappear when he approached. His
relentless questions and requests for justification disempowered
those who reported to him, including those productive members with long histories of expertise and understanding of their
jobs. The area limped along with frustrated supervisors who
dreaded even to listen to their voice mail. They knew their manager's voice would be on the tape questioning things that had
already been done, explaining things they already knew, and
requesting meetings that would be not meetings but lectures
about what he would do if he were doing their jobs. His attempts
to coach or guide seemed to always result in an uproar instead of
improvement in individual and group performance.

This manager appeared frustrated by the negative responses
but could not gain acceptance. The group avoided or rejected his
offers to discuss the situation. He was not a "legitimatized"

leader; members would not, even could not, anoint him as such. The outcome was a lot of wasted technical experience. He had no one with whom to share that experience. He was not a leader.

Working with and leading with co-members throughout the workplace community requires the ability to collaborate, a function of the consultative activity. Positive, productive, connecting relationships are necessary for the Membership Organization to thrive as a top-performance organization. As discussed in Chapter One, membership is an interactive, interdependent, collaborative, *relational* way of working that nurtures inclusion and acceptance. In the Membership Organization, the relational approach focuses on valuing others and creating connections that are enjoyable, beneficial, and significant to the establishment of productive partnerships. Of course, the relational approach must be practiced by all members, no matter where they work in the organizational circle.

In the past, the successful hierarchical leader was driven, controlling, and often feared. Members did as instructed, not connecting or participating across the circle and not participating in decision making. Relationship building was not a priority and was often seen as inappropriate to leadership. Leaders stayed separate from the organizational community, isolated and "dignified." For the members, remaining isolated and disconnected from the leaders was often the best way to work well on the job. Staying in the middle of the pack was safest.

When people began to understand the need for participation in decisioning, organizations began to seek (allow) participation—but often only within limits. They accepted involvement reluctantly and limited it to suggestions that they could in effect ignore—or worse, to what management wanted to hear. The barrier between the "thinkers" and the "doers" was not lowered.

However, in today's more complex organizational environment, the sole leader at the "top" who does all the thinking and deciding no longer exists in most cases. There is not enough time in the day to get all the information, deal with all the issues, and do all the visualizing that is vital to ongoing success. It is now obvious that leading with whole-system involvement, spreading decisioning and accountability to the organization's most energetic, knowledgeable, and proactive members, wherever they are, is significant to top organizational performance. This requires that organizations adopt a new approach and belief system regarding individual member performance, one that focuses on lowering barriers to deep participation. David Noer (1997) says,

> Our leaders have always been cowboys, and still are, it seems. . . . We believe that deeply rooted cultural and social problems can be solved if only we pick the right president. If he (or someday she) does well, we praise him; if not, we blame him, and woe betide him if he proves to have the kind of personal problems that we accept—even defend— in us lesser humans. (p. 165)

The top cowboy can paralyze an organization, slow down accomplishment of goals, and bring spontaneous decisioning and innovation to a standstill. An incident in a small but successful health care organization brought to the forefront what happens when a top cowboy is suddenly gone. The leader was paternalistic and secretive, exercising full control in decisioning down to the smallest detail. The unthinkable happened when the leader was struck with a sudden catastrophic illness and was gone. The organization struggled to transition with little knowledge, leaving the members to observe a new leader who appeared inept, fumbling, and unprepared to lead. The former leader had set him up to fail. By leading with, working with, and working within connected partnering relationships, the Membership Organization takes on a new gestalt.

The Humanization of the Workplace

Leaders of the past were only credible if they were unemotional, secretive, and remote. Often the one emotion they were willing to show was anger, and that was painful. They would say that their door was always open, but if you raised an issue that made them uncomfortable or delivered bad news, you were laying your future on the line. "Relational" interaction was a joke.

The concept of relational organizational leading acknowledges that interactions in the workplace are emotional happenings. Only recently has research focused on feelings and their relationship to performance in the workplace. George and Brief (1996) tell us that "current approaches to motivation neglect the role of feelings" and that "feelings, be they emotions or moods, do not occupy a central role in current theoretic approaches to motivation" (pp. 78–79). Fortunately, recent interest in and study on how we feel about our work, how we "work with," and the impact of "stuff" that happens is coming to the attention of organizational researchers. This new cadre recognizes that we have feelings while working and that those feelings matter. Now they have to convince those who matter—those with whom we work every day.

In dehumanized work environments, management "tells" through actions that feelings are to be ignored, feared, shut down, and set aside. Members identify with the wishes of the leader-group and make choices thought to be appropriate by the leader. In this environment, supervisors and managers may habitually use language and gestures that discount "less-than" organizational members. This signals to others that disconnection is the appropriate way of leading and working. Discounting and disconnection lead to withholding information, criticism, abusiveness, disrespect, and unrealistic expectations by the symbolic leaders. When change is necessary, the actions of the unemotional, even abusive, leader increase resistance and doom the change to failure.

Ira Chaleff (1996) says, "Among the most abusive acts are those committed by leaders who passionately pursue revolutionary social goals, but are incapable of feeling or identifying with the pain of a single individual" (p. 137). For example, a disconnected and ambitious divisional manager "led" the organization into teams. The choice was well meant, but the outcome was less than successful; the manager used tactics of nonsupport, criticism, poor training (if any), and emphasis on the negative as tools for change. Instead of recognizing and emphasizing the positive (increasing feelings of hope), the manager subjected everyone to ridicule, demonstrating how to be "successfully" wrong (and increasing feelings of hopelessness). Often the manager zeroed in on someone who had been accused of somehow wronging a co-worker. Running to the manager with what-is-wrong-today became a way of getting recognition and reward—or revenge for long-past misdeeds. The manager took the targeted offender before a "performance improvement committee." The offender sat on the opposite side of the large conference table from the five members of the committee (top management of the organization). The manager was the spokesperson as the others sat with disapproving, somber expressions watching the responses of the presumably malfunctioning member. It was not a pretty sight—or experience.

As might be expected, the effectiveness of the teams was lower because of competition and discontent. Eventually the "innovator" moved on to another unsuspecting organizational community. The challenge for the new leader of the organization is to get the teams to cooperate rather than compete, connect rather than disconnect, be in relationship rather than isolation—a formidable challenge of recovery from "innovative leadership."

The effective relational leader recognizes that demonstrated, real, meaningful, and connecting empathy and sincerity lead to successful, quality interpersonal relationships. The abusive, disconnected, autocratic manager and leader destroys hope, which can survive only through positive interpersonal relationship and interrelatedness in the workplace—nurtured by emotional connections made through the relational approach. Sustainability requires organizations to humanize how members are treated. The trade-off is that members participate more effectively and more willingly in constructing a successful organization.

Organizational Climate

The general systems model of organizational functioning represents that "organizationwide conditions and practices referred to as organizational climate, along with other more group-specific contextual factors, shape the behavior of the members of a work group" (Denison, 1990, pp. 42–43). Membership addresses the importance of the symbolic nature of organizational life. Each member connects unconsciously to the values and beliefs of the organization and to the climate surrounding the meaning systems. Daniel Denison (1990), when designing a survey on organizational culture and effectiveness (see Chart 12 on page 100), included questions pertaining to organizational climate.

CHART 12   Organizational Climate Index

- *Organization of work.*
  The degree to which an organization's work methods link the jobs of individuals to organizational objectives.

- *Communication flow.*
  The flow of information, both vertically within the organizational hierarchy and laterally across the organization.

- *Emphasis on people.*
  The interest that the organization displays in the welfare and development of the people who work there.

- *Decision-making practices.*
  The degree to which an organization's decisions involve those who will be affected, are made at appropriate levels, and are based on widely shared information.

- *Influence and control.*
  The influence of those at the [edges of the circle].

- *Absence of bureaucracy.*
  The absence of unnecessary administrative constraints in the organization's internal functioning.

- *Coordination.*
  Coordination, cooperation, and problem resolution among organizational units.

Note: From D. R. Denison (1990), *Corporate Culture and Organizational Effectiveness* pp. 43–44. Reprinted with permission.

It is unavoidable that an organization would have a way of dealing with interpersonal relationships that is tried and true, developed over the long term. The leaders of the organization control this through rules, procedures, rewards, and recognition. The perceptions and reactions of the individual member are an outcome of the climate of the organization. What members do and say are choices, but they are also the result of perceptions of and reactions to the conditions in which the organizational member has been socialized. Although leader-members are largely responsible for the formation of the climate by the controls imposed, it is in the best interest of the leader to create rules that are connected to the beliefs, assumptions, values, and relationships that are important to the members and their perceptions of how to be effective on the job, as well as to the values significant to achievement of the organization's purpose.

Although there is some disagreement regarding the significance of the organization's climate to the success of the organization, it is clear that the history and current environment of the organization can affect the performance of the individual and the collective membership. Leader-members ignore the climate of the workplace to the peril of the organization.

But responsibility for the climate of the organization does not stop at the center of the circle. In the Membership Organization, community members share the responsibility to support and encourage an organizational climate that is positive, productive, respectful, and challenging. Otherwise negativity can become contagious, passing from person to person and from department to department. Soon the organization loses energy and the pace of achievement slows.

In an organizational climate of relational membership, there is less pain, which permits the formation of partnerships across blurred lines in the circle and allows empowerment to flourish; feelings of contribution, significance, and connection lower barriers of defensiveness.

Relational Membership

In Membership Organizations, members *intentionally* accept the responsibility to establish effective relationships, making emotion-based decisions about the energy they expend on their work. Interdependent relationships allow participants to create partnerships, contribute to the best of their ability, and be empowered, taking the challenges offered through deep participation.

The word *intentionally* indicates that partnering relationships and deep participation do not happen without commitment. In today's complex world, members make choices regarding involvements on and off the job. Working in an organization that diffuses accountabilities across the organization requires all members to establish relationships that support setting appropriate priorities, gathering needed information, and empowering decisioning. Relationships are important both on and off the job. The nature of work may be changing, but the need to connect and interact productively at work is stronger than ever.

CHART 13   Relational Membership

■ *Increases the member's ability to cope with uncertainty.*
While increased information, open communication, and increased
involvement in organizational issues create uncertainty, they also
offers opportunities for the member to understand. With openness,
uncertainty can be acknowledged and dealt with. Knowledge creates
opportunities to cope with the known, not fear the unknown.

■ *Increases hope.*
Membership Organizations make it possible to be more hopeful.
Optimism and perception of a better working environment increase
energy and open opportunities for innovation and creativity, positively affecting the human and financial bottom lines of the organization.

■ *Increases information flow.*
Members are more open to listening, sharing information, and seeking information within the group and across the organizational circle. Lowering boundaries eliminates some of the risk of getting input
and lessens the need to duplicate work, prove a point, or withhold
information. The organizational community is more accepting
of the common goals and more willing to work together to reach
those goals.

■ *Increases reframing.*
Seeing (perceiving) our organization and our relationships with internal and external customers through new lenses makes it possible to
frame disruptions as learning events. Always digging for the dirt is
destructive. Purposeful awareness of the "good" increases member
willingness to contribute and lead when opportunities arise.

■ *Decreases defensiveness.*
Being open to constructive accountability and challenge (questioning) provides opportunities for growth and achievement. Defensive
reasoning, the act of justifying, is self-protective and causes disconnections in relationships. Defensiveness leads to misunderstandings, distortions, and self-fulfilling and self-sealing processes
(Argyris, 1990). Of course, organizations with defensive members
have cynical members who are actively putting up barriers to
"constructive consultation."

No longer are people focused on doing just what is in front of
them. They must be aware of the impact of their work on those
around them and take responsibility for their own actions and
behaviors. Choices must be intentional. All members are part of
something bigger than their own work. Relational membership
requires extra effort. In the Membership Organization, people care

whether others are upset or if there is something they can do to be more productive. The relational approach changes the nature of how people work as a community. When relationships are built on open cooperation, acceptance, and inclusion, more open interactions follow and defensiveness decreases, as seen in Chart 13.

To understand the effect of relational membership, look around. In a relational membership environment, (1) the elements of active communication, shared learning, and distributed accountability exist; (2) members are encouraged to exercise influence through high levels of responsibility and to challenge status quo on a regular basis; and (3) members throughout the circle support and encourage an organizational climate that is positive, productive, respectful, and challenging. These elements deliver the message that "we are the organization" and "we can only do this together."

Communication

The more open, relational member has an ability to communicate genuine caring, concern, and enthusiasm to co-members across the organizational circle. Seeing and appreciating others as performers who contribute beneficial actions and attitudes to the organizational community increase feelings of competence, empowerment, and involvement on the job. Because the lines are blurred, members throughout the circle actively affect the performance of others. Consciously or unconsciously, members give signals regarding significance or nonsignificance. Through believable relationship-building gestures, all members tell one another that they believe in their co-members and the organization.

Learning

Formal leaders model and validate methods of connecting and influencing to create an environment in which all members can learn and grow. But today's organizational realities combine learning and employability and place the responsibility for these knowledge growth elements on the shoulders of the individual member. When members accept learning as a responsibility and act on it, that makes them employable in the future—no matter where they work in the circle. Employability is its own leveling device, affecting member opportunities now and in the future.

An organizational investment is also essential. Organizations, to remain competitive and innovative, require everyone to be alert to and listen to education and training needs and require that both the individual and the organization actively invest in member competence. Individual competence is an investment in the future of the organization. Ultimately, investment in employability of the individual multiplies to strengthen the success potential of the organization. When the collective membership is prepared to take on challenging work, members' feelings of competence and significance grow, contributing to the success of empowerment initiatives.

When the organization is willing to invest in the member, other circumstances aside, the member is more likely to be committed to the organization for a longer time. Organizational survival requires development of knowledge, skills, and abilities. Personal mastery of work skills and expansion of capabilities encourage uninhibited and innovative investment of energies in times of stress, chaos, and ambiguity. A lowered sense of capability and mastery disempowers and disengages members. As Harry Levinson says (1968, p. 201), "The less the sense of mastery, the more likely is there to be organizational passivity." To be a passive organization with passive employees is to fail.

Accountability

In the Membership Organization, decisioning opportunities and accountabilities are spread across the organization to the members closest to the location of the decision. Members throughout the organization are active decisioning agents. Accountability for performance of the overall organization is now spread to the edges of the circle, as we will discuss further in Chapter Seven. Each member must contribute, accepting personal responsibility for creating beneficial relationships that support the work. This carries with it assumptions of top performance as a requirement for personal success.

Working relationally requires that each member support efforts toward improvement by others who are struggling. Improving skills is a challenge, and support must be readily offered. Patience is significant to the improvement process—for both the member working to make improvements and those coaching and supporting the improvement effort.

Influencing

The Membership Organization encourages influencing, an element of the consultative role of members. Through appreciation of the knowledge, accomplishments, and differences of organizational members, influencing spreads to the edges, increasing the effectiveness of all members.

Implicit in the relational approach is the willingness of all members to support actions of influencing. Successful influencing requires participation of two or more people. It is a partnership or group activity, encouraging new viewpoints, directions, and instances of innovation, creativity, and connections. Leader willingness to stay out of the way when partnerships of influencing are working well—but without disappearing and reappearing only when there is a mistake or trouble in the wind—is significant to the success of overall membership influencing tactics. (An atmosphere that encourages influencing means that the leader-member has the ability to balance being present and being absent while appreciating the influencing gestures of the members.) Eric H. Neilsen (1986) discusses influencing tactics of the appreciative leader, but these same tactics are important to all members to influence their organization:

> Leading appreciatively involves the use of influence tactics such as *nurturing* (listening actively, empathizing with others' experience, assuring others of their strengths and competence, offering trust in others' decisions about their own choices) and *applauding* (acknowledging ways in which other members have helped one personally; praising members as individuals, not just their performance, in front of their colleagues; using terms of friendship). (p. 93; Neilsen's italics)

Examples of influencing include joining teams to share information and expertise; seeking knowledge from the budget coordinator when funding is being sought for a project; giving and receiving input from a member or members in another area as to what can be done to improve acceptance rates when a product moves to their area; sharing information and potential solutions received from an internal or external customer regarding a concern; and constructing a mutually beneficial data base so input from all stakeholders is available to all parties. Also, openly acknowledging the input of others on a project is an important influencing action.

Member influencing activities can increase individual member credibility, create opportunities for involvement, and expand learning for the group. Influencing also establishes connections, partnerships, alliances, and inter- and intragroup opportunities for higher performance and innovation, making it possible to examine and challenge the status quo. Successfully challenging the status quo creates uncertainty. But working in a relational community reinforces member tolerances, expanding comfort zones of understanding that contribute to reducing uncertainty and creating a safer environment for empowerment, input, and change. The need for change is inevitable. In the relational community, the organizational climate supports influencing activities of examining, recognizing, acknowledging, challenging, and supporting those needed changes.

The Connecting Process of Membership

Connecting is relational. In a Membership Organization, the establishment of successful relationships is the responsibility of every member, adding energy to the individual, the group, and the organization.

Establishing relational connections is a dynamic, reciprocal, and risk-taking process. Members feel an urgency to establish connections that produce meaningful work (to make a difference) and to have healthy relationships with the people around them (to enjoy their work) (Bracey & Smith, 1992). If members cannot achieve desirable and comfortable relational connections, that limits their ability to enjoy meaningful work. The process is illustrated in Figure 2.

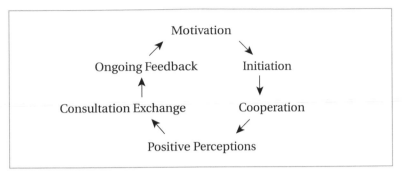

FIGURE 2   The Connecting Process

The connecting process starts with the individual being *motivated* to *initiate* a relationship with the team or group. Motivation to do so leads to a willingness to *cooperate* and collaborate with the members of the group, encourages *positive perceptions* of participants in the process, is built on continued evaluation or *consultation exchange,* and provides *ongoing feedback* to participants that the relationship is beneficial and acceptable. Connection is a result of the establishment of good relationships, and the process is reactivated with each additional encounter.

Motivation

Beneficial connections across the workplace circle are important to the individual, the group, and the organization. It is no surprise that connections will not happen unless the individual is motivated to connect. Relational beings (all humans are relational to some degree) need the support, assurance, and acknowledgment of those around them—the people they sense are significant to their well-being. Without the desire for connection, members are not likely to make it happen.

The first level of motivation is doing something out of *fear:* I have to do this or else. Whether conscious or unconscious, this is a powerful reactionary emotion.

The second level of motivation is *duty:* I ought to do this. This is the result of being assigned accountability and is more fulfilling than fear, although doing something out of duty gets burdensome after a while.

The third level of motivation is *wanting:* I want to do this. The member is eager, inspired, and comfortable with the idea. The outcome of wanting is *doing*. The member is determined to make this work.

Although there are organizational (situational) and relational issues that affect a member's motivation, members ultimately motivate themselves. The desire to perform enhances or undermines top performance and contributes to feelings of competence, empowerment, challenge, and significance. Nadler and Lawler (1995) state that motivation is "the force on the individual to expand effort. . . . Performance results from a combination of the effort that an individual puts forth *and* the level of ability that he or she has (reflecting skills, training, information, etc.). As a result of performance, the individual attains . . . outcomes" (p. 30).

When motivated, members are energized and hopeful; they feel that what they are doing is worthwhile and right and purposeful. Thus they have a sense of accomplishment, ownership, and self-worth as well as potential recognition and support (provided by co-members).

Employees who have a resistant mind-set may or may not enjoy themselves as they are. If they do, it will take a sledgehammer to even get their attention—but it is possible. Leaving them alone is a signal that their resistance is acceptable. Such employees routinely resist every new thing that is or may be beneficial to the company. Eventually they will attract others to their cause, and they can affect the performance of everyone with whom they come in contact. They look for allies on and off the job, constantly seeking others to share their stuck attitudes and behaviors. Their "ain't it awful" mind-set (see Figure 3, p. 117) clouds issues and affects the motivation of those around them. Of course, adding this individual to an already high-performing team can be disastrous. Not addressing this person's negative effect can eventually affect the social, human, and financial bottom lines of the organization.

Connection is short term and situational, requiring the desire to continually nurture relationships with co-members and customers. Meaningful work and healthy relationships that flow from comfortable connections require ongoing involvement in keeping those connections alive; they cannot be taken for granted and can be broken easily. Co-member (internal customer) and external customer relationships can fragment quickly, even instantaneously, as a result of negative feelings and responses. Maintaining positive connections requires us to be aware, alert, and proactive in working relationships with others.

Initiation

Initiating connections means engaging in behaviors that provide opportunities and justifications for relationships. It means going the extra mile, accepting a secondary role in the success of co-members, and offering others a role in successful endeavors. It means being willing to initiate opportunities to be consultative. Finally, it means performing in ways that can contribute to both self-success and the success of others while also adding value to the bottom lines of the organization. When members initiate connections, they establish opportunities for synergistic relationships of potential value and importance—to the partners involved and to the organization.

Cooperation

Members seek opportunities for cooperative and supportive relationships with others. Constructive cooperation includes input from all of the involved co-members. To quote a friend's metaphor, friendship (connections) is built on participants both giving to and taking from a "basket full of favors." The basket is filled at the time when the connection (friendship) is established, when both are unconsciously deciding what can and cannot be done to maintain the connection. Over time, each will put in and take out as needed. Caring and cooperation nurture the ebb and flow. When one is putting in and the other is only taking out, there is disconnection. In the working community, too, when one person is taking advantage, the relationship disintegrates and cooperation can turn into competition. The positive participation of both parties is significant to the success of the relational partnership.

Positive Perceptions

Often what we see is what we get at work and what we see is based on perceptions and assumptions that shape member attitudes on the job. Often, perceptions of fairness or unfairness result in positive or negative connecting behaviors and thus in connection or disconnection. Consciously or unconsciously, members decide which actions to take and what responses to make in connecting or disconnecting with those around them. These actions and responses send their message loud and clear.

There are all-too-common responses today in work communities that demonstrate negative perceptions and disconnections. The "that's-not-my-job" syndrome automatically identifies the employee as not being a contributing member of the organization. These members nurse their negative perceptions and avoid positive connections in order to avoid deeper involvement. Energized members who are willing to make the effort to initiate connections are not content with minimal involvement or mediocre performance, nor are these members content to merely watch others contribute.

Consultation Exchange

Successful members initiate and build solid relationships through exchanges of information. These participants are constantly on the alert for constructive evaluation and feedback in order to effectively maintain positive working relationships. Effective evaluation and feedback is a consultation exchange—an opportunity for participants to learn together what makes a good working relationship. It is an exchange of information that builds connection instead of competition. All participants automatically evaluate their relationships.

Evaluations tell the individual that relationship situations are (1) fair, neutral, or unfair; and (2) beneficial, neutral, or not beneficial. The fair and beneficial connections will be nurtured. Feedback through consultation exchanges is based on concern for the welfare of the connected person; is constructive; and will be accepted. Neutral exchanges will seem unreliable when the chips are down and will be tested occasionally, putting distance between the participants. In such cases, members will give consultation feedback only as necessary, with reluctance. Withholding and nonacceptance will be practiced by both participants.Of course, relationships that are seen as unfair and not beneficial bring disconnection and strong resistance to working together.

Ongoing Feedback

Positive, ongoing feedback as an extension of the consultative exchange allows members to hear new viewpoints and address positive and conflictive understandings and misunderstandings. Ongoing feedback actively addresses appreciation and nonappreciation of situations within a partnership or community. Interdependence and effective collaboration depend on ongoing feedback occurring back and forth across the circle—requiring all members to participate in the process. Wherever the members perform in the circle, such feedback is a membership task that must be undertaken in a way that strengthens connections and increases responder motivation, consistently contributing to the connecting process.

The connecting process revitalizes connections, inviting and increasing member involvement to move beyond participation. The motivation to maintain partnerships that are productive and supportive is nurtured by connections that consistently occur across the workplace community.

Connected Partnerships

The relational approach is the basis for top-performing partnerships between two or more members. The inclusiveness value in the Membership Organization stresses that partnerships are important to the success of the individual and the organization. Across organizations, effective blurred-line partnerships flourish. The secretary who partners with her leader in the "flow" of how things are accomplished in a working-with atmosphere expands the influence of both partners. The customer contact

> **CHART 14   Connected Partnerships**
>
> - Are professional
> - Are alert to exchanges
> - Are knowledgeable
> - Take notice
> - Add value to the organization
> - Take calculated risks

person who actively addresses customer issues *on the spot* is partnering with the customer to address issues of concern. The leader-member who seeks active involvement of the members in their areas of expertise in decisioning is creating partnerships. Complex issues become more understandable when effective, empowered partnerships occur. Successful empowerment initiatives also must provide opportunity for members to link with others with complementary abilities. As seen in Chart 14, in the most productive partnerships, members:

Are professional. Because members are representatives of the organization, co-members and customers expect them to be professional. Of course, *professionalism* means something different in each industry, but there are some common denominators: courtesy, appropriate language, sharing of common goals, performance, adherence to cultural norms, and appropriate interpersonal activities.

Are alert to exchanges. Members watch for positive or negative exchanges in partnerships. Feeling and showing concern when co-members and partners are feeling vulnerable is important to getting past it and reestablishing feelings of well-being. No one works in a vacuum. Mutual concern is part of feeling connected, worthwhile, and significant. Of course, fundamental to the relational approach is each member focusing on having discipline (disciplining oneself to think about what is happening and its impact on others in the organization) rather than on doing discipline (judging the actions and activities of others and attempting to do something about those behaviors).

Are knowledgeable. Whether sitting at desks or standing at machines, members do not turn off their brains when they go to work in the morning. When a member's knowledge or sense of order indicates that something is amiss or something is important, he or she investigates and raises a flag of concern, confirming the commitment to doing things right and heightening feelings of connection and involvement. That member thereby establishes credibility and a reputation for being knowledgeable about his or her work. Sharing knowledge also establishes productive agreements with co-members, expanding and building the knowledge base of the membership.

Take notice. Being alert to what is happening provides opportunities for top performance. Awareness is a key ingredient of serendipitous decisioning (discussed in Chapter Four) and opportunities for innovative contribution (discussed in Chapter Two). For a partner, active participation involves being open to and participating in consultation exchanges that can benefit the partnership. Consultation exchanges also provide openings for offering information and making constructive contributions to the success of co-members and other partnerships, while expanding possibilities of performance individually and in partnership in the future.

Add value to the organization. Connections allow members to add value to their workplace community by opening channels of communication. Members learn from, innovate with, contribute to, and energize those around them. A member's willingness and ability to add value to his or her assigned areas of accountability affect the status quo or static stance of the organization. Through those areas of accountability members can add value to their group and organization. Partnerships can move whole industries—and more. Positive, productive partnering connections influence all three bottom lines. Members decide together the growability and survivability of their organization.

Take calculated risks. Innovation and creativity increase growth and survival potential for members and their organization. Taking well-thought-out risks also keeps the excitement of involvement alive in the group. Working in a dull organization is deadly for an action-oriented member. Sooner or later, this member creates excitement—and it may or may not be a positive contribution to the organization. Appropriate risk taking challenges and invigorates connected, productive, empowered partnerships.

The Limits of Being Relational

An issue in the workplace today, and most significant to the survivability of organizations, is the propensity of individuals, on and off the job, to distrust and disbelieve. It is often automatic to start from the prove-it-to-me, give-me-a-reason-to-care, or so-what-have-you-done-for-me-lately orientation. Robert M. D'Aprix (1976) expresses it quite effectively by stating, "There is abroad a feeling which pollster Daniel Yankelovich bluntly describes as the 'bullshit syndrome.' It is the credibility gap at its worst, the kind of distrust which leads people to respond to some message not with 'Is that so?' but with 'Bullshit!'" (p. 27).

Although D'Aprix wrote about this in the 1970s, little has improved. The increase in cynicism and distrust makes this response even more prevalent today. Unfortunately this cynicism is the biggest threat to even the most successful leadership group's ability to turn around lagging organizations. Without the enrollment of the employees, struggling organizations are doomed. When members dig in their heels and say bullshit!, nothing will stop the organization's downfall: Cutting back, selling off, or shutting down will be the only solutions. To do otherwise requires the buy-in of the members. So leaders struggle to revive a dying organization as it is symbolically holding its nose for the downward plunge. At such times, new and innovative ways of working cannot occur. When no one is listening to one another, everyone blames. The politics of individual survival, self-protection, and self-promotion create barriers to working through the crisis.

As previously noted, some members have an overwhelming need for their organizations to be perfect, for everything that is done to be perfectly fair to everyone. This implies that (1) everyone should get what he or she wants; (2) imperfect people should not be forgiven; (3) if it doesn't work for me, it's not right for anyone; and (4) the organization and its representatives are automatically to be discounted and distrusted. For such people, perfection is the yardstick for acceptance and approval.

Perfection expectancy is manifested in various ways. It is shown by members who expect their leaders to know what their needs are—automatically. It occurs with members who are impatient for results and with leader-members who expect their co-members to be patient—without informing them of their rationale. Unforgiving team members who expect their team to leap into cohesiveness instead of going through normal stages of team development are expecting perfection, as are customer contact members who expect customers to follow all the rules—all the time. The list is endless. Although all of us share some expectation of perfection regarding the things we care about, multiple members carrying this expectation to extreme is deadly to the connection process and to partnerships in the workplace community.

Unfortunately, multiple versions of members with perfection expectancy may appear in the group that is taking a relational approach. These people may actively victimize relationally oriented co-members and leader-members. Efforts at accountability may or may not get results, but if these people are not held accountable, it will be noticed by co-members. In some organizations, the counterculture may be detrimental to the membership process. Although it is theoretically possible to bring everyone into the membership stance, the probability is low. In some instances, personal change will have to be encouraged, supported, even demanded. It should be noted here that the Membership Organization makes room for contributors who prefer a more solitary way of working—those not cut out for teams. There are contributive, motivated, functional members who work better on their own. These members work hard all day, contributing to the welfare of the community in a way that is different from that of others. As long as a member is adding value, he or she should be supported.

Personal Change

Counterculture members are purposefully cynical about anything the organizational leaders and co-members might be attempting to achieve. Whatever is happening, it's wrong. Whatever is requested is wrong. Whatever is represented as possible is wrong. However, some organizations are unwilling to hold these members accountable. Ryan and Oestreich (1991) tell us,

> If you really want to create a quality organization, certain behaviors must stop. There is a time and a place for establishing requirements, not just goals. Additionally . . . it is good to keep in mind the phrase: "The whole world is watching." How you treat people who do not match the standard will probably be considered by others in the organization the greatest test of your ability to match your actions to your words. You must deal with obvious interpersonal problems if you want to maintain credibility as a leader. (p. 148)

Hammond and Overton (1995) note that an individual's response to a potential change may be one of surprise. Even when there have been warnings that there may be a better way of doing things or an external threat that potentially could bring the need for change, these members may tend to ignore, deny, and wish away the significance of the unknown.

For example, members may be asked to participate in partnerships across organizational boundaries when they have not done so before (see Figure 3). First, they become alert to what is happening. Then they check it out and ask themselves, What is this new way I'm supposed to do things? This may or may not be an acknowledgment of accepting partnership as beneficial. Their level of investment may be balanced by the amount of knowledge and information they have regarding this new method of working together.

If members have some understanding of how partnership works, they may compare the new way to the old way, allowing themselves to consider the change. They may check how much time and energy will be required to understand, or they may check what capabilities they need in order to be successful in the new way of doing things.

They ask themselves, Am I willing to try this new way of working together? Their decision may be personal and definitive, or it

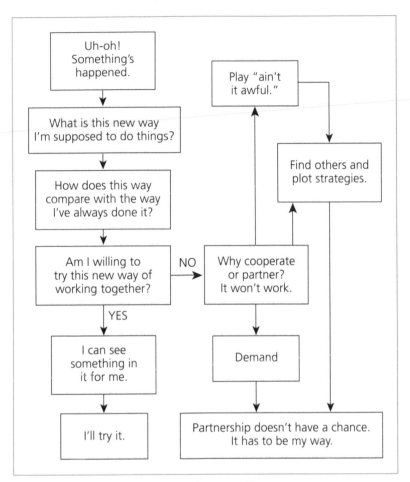

FIGURE 3   Considering Partnership as a Change

Note: Adapted from S. Hammond & M. Overton (1995), *Lake Miramar's Change Model.* Reprinted with permission.

may be influenced by someone they respect. If the people promoting the partnership are not respected, they will have a negative influence; their promotion of the partnership will evoke an automatic no. Of course, if the new way of working is on a member's own wish list, he or she will be willing to make the needed investments of time, energy, and enthusiasm in accepting the proposed opportunity.

If the member's decision is yes, the partnership has a chance. The member's acceptance influences his or her willingness to work at putting the change into place. If the decision is no, the member will wish for the proposed partnership to disappear and will (1) ignore it (he or she may go through the training, but just as a "tourist," not planning to actually invest energy in learning to use the skills being offered); (2) find people who will listen and play "ain't it awful" (he or she shames, points fingers, attacks those who made the decisions regarding the partnership, and plots no-change strategies); and, if there is an active counterculture, (3) plot efforts to delay, manipulate, sabotage, and eliminate the impending partnership.

Such members may, through controlling change potential over time, actually close down the organization—and feel justified in doing so, still blaming and attacking because "they" didn't do what was necessary to turn the organization around. These members do not believe in shared accountability. It's all "their" fault.

In the past, organizations typically tolerated such members if their opinions did not get in the way of work or incite others to challenge the status quo (Parenti, 1978). Keeping things the same worked well. In the Membership Organization, if the member is not a contributing member, the organization has the responsibility to encourage, even demand, increased contribution through coaching, challenging, setting specific expectations, peer training, and specific education. Challenging the performance of the member in this way expands possibilities for change. Relational leading includes the responsibility to encourage and coach these members to re-enroll through personal change. Although de-enrolling (firing) a member is counter to the relational approach, sometimes it must be done. Keeping this member is nonproductive for the organization and prevents the member from finding a "fit" elsewhere.

Summary

Members throughout the new community are experiencing a sense of risk and vulnerability that calls for connections not previously possible in the bureaucratic organizational environment. Work arrangements are changing, requiring different sets of relationships. The relational approach to membership in the organizational community allows for productive interactions of formal/informal leading and deep participation/enrollment by all members. These actions contribute to the success of the overall organization and to blurring the lines across the circle.

Where the relational approach is alive and well, formal and informal leader-members initiate, model, coach, and expect their co-members to lead, extending leadership and accountability for the success of the organization to the edges of the circle. These new expectations of top performance become integrated into the Membership Organization. In order to distribute accountability and leadership across the organizational circle to members willing to be top performers, the more level circle of membership is essential—leading with and working with must happen with all members.

6

Make no mistake about it: people have very high expectations of their leaders. [Members] are more demanding and harder to please than ever these days. They are also very disappointed. The heroic leadership myth has been shattered, and cynicism has taken its place. But people still want and need leadership. . . . They want leaders who will put principles ahead of politics and other people before self-interests.

James M. Kouzes and Barry Z. Posner, *Credibility: How Leaders Gain and Lose It, Why People Demand It*

PRINCIPLE 5

Leadership

> Chosen, assigned leader-
> members still lead. Leader-
> ship happens at all levels,
> and every member has the
> potential to be a catalyst for
> achievement and an agent
> for change.

After working for old-style leaders, I eventually worked for a more casual, open, relational leader, who often chatted casually with members at all levels, asking questions, telling stories and laughing, discussing family, and arguing for his favorite football team (the Pittsburgh Steelers). The members were not used to this kind of leadership. Some were concerned about his relaxed demeanor: Would this informality get in the way of leadership? At first wary, they were soon converted; his relational leading style was partnered with visionary, knowledge-based skills, which made him a credible leader. When he left, members hoped his successor would be at least a little like him. Sadly, his leadership style was not successfully replaced. His successor feigned it for a while, but soon she was recognized as one of the command-and-control-type leaders.

Even in the best organizations, there are a lot of angry employees. Some employees say that this anger is a result of the organizational structures they must contend with and the leadership styles they are forced to work "under." Bureaucratic, hierarchical organizations that promote cultures in which people at the top think, and people at the bottom do—with as little inter-action as possible—perpetuate dependency, magnify the frustrations of members, and keep them-versus-us relationships in place. Members all across the circle have psychological responses to these inept, ineffective structures, management styles, and processes that generate the sense that the organization is out of control.

The Functions of Leadership

The membership concept recognizes the need for selected, legitimate leader-members who are charged with being alert to the overall welfare of the organization; they will not be replaced by the larger group. (Common thinking in Western culture is that someone has to sit where the buck stops.) In order to maintain certain core competencies, organizations will retain some structure. Workplace communities will take steps to become more flexible and dynamic to meet the ebb and flow of the more chaotic business climate of today (Brousseau, Driver, Eneroth, & Larsson, 1996). Although members are all accountable for the success or failure of their organizations, as we will discuss further in Chapter Seven, some members perform in the formal leadership role and others as informal leaders on an ongoing basis. Formal leaders encourage their co-members to be deeply involved and actively support others in the initiative, thus performing as linking mechanisms in the organization. Their efforts to promote connecting partnerships across the organization facilitate the possibility of an energized and responsible workplace community. As these relational leaders serve as linking agents, their influence (positive or negative), wherever they are in the organization, affects the language and interchange of the overall community.

Leadership Tactics

Leadership tactics cover a wide range of styles, and what may be viewed as "the best" today can cause disaster tomorrow.

One thing is constant: Members at all levels of the company are "thinkers" and "doers" who make it possible or impossible for organizations to accomplish. There is no one member level that alone can make the organization successful. Leaders, as co-members, exist to serve the organization and its members. They are a merged stakeholder group inside the organization.

Leaders, as members, constantly strive to support, encourage, and benefit all members. All organizational levels reciprocate with enhancing gestures and activities leading to mutual achievement in the workplace. If the members succeed, the organization succeeds. If they fail, the organization fails. Members throughout the more level circle are intertwined and interdependent, as discussed in Chapter Four.

Because of this interdependence and co-membership, when leaders lead, they do so in ways that enable everyone to exercise their best membership tactics. Leaders actively influence positive and effective member participation in the organization. Leaders encourage all members to use their expertise and empowerment, no matter where they are positioned, to the benefit of the organization. Leaders listen and act when experts suggest creative innovations. Leaders eliminate barriers that limit member abilities to meet personal goals and the goals of group and organization. Leaders are willing to provide appropriate resources, recognition, and rewards for member involvement and commitment to the organization. As stated by William Plamondon (1996), "Leaders generate energy—and pass it on."

Members respond to people, situations, and processes. One very important catalyst for response is the way members perceive they are being treated. Many years ago, unions were organized primarily to balance management's control over employees (Levinson, 1968). Eventually it became obvious that leader power was only possible when followers consented to it. Effectiveness of the manager was the focus at that time; the "how to" of managing meant knowing what to do when, giving orders, and being tough. The success or failure of the organization rested on the shoulders of management. Members waited to be told what to do.

Since the 1930s, the evolution from management to leadership has led to a relationship of (1) personality, (2) the "followers," (3) the organization, and (4) the working environment. We now know that leadership tactics directly affect high performance at all levels (Brion, 1996). A leader's willingness and ability to listen to, respond to, provide resources for, and inform co-members on a continuing basis affect bottom lines. Successful leadership is now a partnership with members all across the organizational circle.

Relational Leadership

Strong, relational leaders keep members focused and involved and encourage deep participation in running the organization. Such leaders take a "leading with" approach to working with members located at every level of the organization. Leading-with leader-members enable others and are recognized by their willingness to ask, involve, empower, and encourage members at all levels to partner in achievement, both individually and organizationally. The leading-with leader recognizes that what all members do and what all members say is important to the organization's success and shares that knowledge with them.

Relational leadership is based on the belief that the organization's future is dependent on relationships—both within the organization and between organizational participants and those external to the organization. Thus relational leadership emphasizes mutual learning, the sharing of knowledge and opinions, cooperation, teamwork, mutual appreciation, and distributed accountability. Relational leading enables members to connect, influence, and participate in the co-construction of futures for themselves, their group, and their organization (thanks for input from Sherene Zolno, The Leading Clinic™, and Kenneth J. Gergen).

In an environment of relational leading, (1) the elements of active communication, shared learning, and appropriate accountability are part of the organizational environment; (2) we are encouraged to exercise influence through high levels of responsibility exercised through our accountabilities and to challenge the status quo on a regular basis; and (3) members at all levels support and encourage an organizational climate that is positive, productive, respectful, and challenging. These elements deliver to all members the relational leader's message that we can only do this together.

Communication, Learning, and Accountability

The more open, relational leader has the ability to communicate genuine, believable caring, concern, and enthusiasm to members at all levels. Seeing and rewarding members' beneficial actions and attitudes increase feelings of competence and significance on the job. Relational leaders demonstrate their belief in their co-members' ability and willingness to support the organization to top performance.

It is important to emphasize that relational leading is not a method of "getting my own way." Positive, productive relationships mean "getting *our* way." Shared, purposeful, relational leadership exhibits consistent beliefs and expectations, which allow, even require, intentional flexibility and accountability of the individual member and the group as a whole. The outcome is a more cooperative, linked, participative membership that is also relational. Mutual cooperation encourages members to share accountabilities for the success of the organizational community.

Research says that when stress and ambiguity are present in the workplace, members revert to wanting highly structured leader behavior (House & Baetz, 1990). It is the wise leader who, even though members are demanding management instead of leadership, knows that when the leader takes full decision-making responsibility, that leader is denying members the opportunity to build foundations for self-respect and security.

An example of a regression to structural behavior is the company in the opening vignette. This company was going through relentless, stressful change. One of the changes was the move to a team structure. The members were unsure of their new roles; chaos prevailed. Members were asked to write reports they did not know how to write, draw up budgets without a clue where to start, and maintain intergroup relationships when conflict was rampant and unaddressed. Former supervisors were sitting on the sidelines, having been told to "stay out of the way and don't manage"—not sure what was expected of them in the new group process and afraid to step out of line for fear of being called before the dreaded productivity improvement committee.

Anxiety was high. This was the time for strong, relational leadership, leading through support, not disempowerment. True to the tendency to revert to helplessness, some members sought leader interventions for intra- and intergroup conflicts. A relational response would have offered training and encouragement to work together to solve issues. The teams would have become more interconnected, more confident in their abilities to deal with conflict on their own, and perhaps more credible in the eyes of the leadership team. Sadly, the leader actively intervened, keeping the teams dependent on top management (pseudo-teams). The leader "fixed" relationships by dictating what was to be done while not always seeking full information. The supervisors had been removed with no effective team process in sight—and replaced with one "top supervisor" who said only "Go be a team." But how? Paralysis and frustration were inevitable. An effective participative process requires extensive training and the utilization of skills across all levels—supervisor and group member alike learning new ways of working together. Cooperation and partnership do not "just happen" in an organization that has existed for decades on the basis of control and delegation.

Leader-members must model and validate connecting with and influencing co-members in an environment in which all can learn and grow. Today's organizational realities combine learning and employability and place the responsibility for these knowledge growth elements on both participants, the member and the organization. In the past, many members would sit through training because it was mandatory or recommended, but they turned their minds off and thought about other things. Accepting learning as a responsibility and acting on it makes it possible for members to be employable in the future—a catalyst to the need to stay alert to the education and training being offered, as discussed in Chapter Three.

If an organization is to remain competitive and innovative, leader-members must seek out and listen to member-identified education and training needs and then actively invest in those needs. Membership competence is an investment in the future. It affects the success of empowerment initiatives, expands the ability for the member to take on challenging work, and contributes to the member's feelings of significance. Also, as discussed in Chapter Three, in an atmosphere in which the organization is willing to invest in the member, other circumstances aside, the member is more likely to be committed to the organization for a longer time.

The leader knows survival requires development of knowledge, skills, and abilities, for both the leader and the co-members. Mastery of work skills encourages uninhibited and innovative investment of energies in times of stress, chaos, and ambiguity. It is not appropriate, even during difficult times, to disempower and disengage members by making unavailable the skills or knowledge they need to succeed. If the leaders don't care about member competence, the members ask themselves, why should I?

An important function of leadership is to develop within the organization a common understanding about the organizational world in which the members work (Pfeffer, 1981). This requires contact, connection, presence, and open discussion. A common understanding cannot be reached and uncertainty cannot be addressed if no information is being shared. Managers who stay in their offices and do not actively connect with their co-workers when uncertainties exist send a message that they do not care about their co-members; connections fragment (if they ever existed) and trust disintegrates. Open discussion of issues eliminates insecurities and, when problems occur, offers opportunities for input and empowerment.

Complexities of Relational Leadership

In the cynical organization, members have high expectations of leaders and are attentive to their level of perfection, possibly waiting for the misstep or missed cue that verifies the leader is just like all the rest. Of course, whether it is said aloud or not, the members are looking for a relational leader—someone willing to link to their individual needs as well as to the workplace community as a whole.

The term *relational* implies a leader who is always kind, always listening, and always caring about each member of the workplace community. These unrealistic expectations add to the already superhuman challenges faced by the organizational leader, wherever he or she works in the organization.

Challenges

Certain challenges are specific to leadership. In a Membership Organization these include (1) gaining and retaining the competencies needed to be a leader in a "beyond participation" organization; (2) successfully dealing with past, present, and future organizational strategies; (3) hiring, sponsoring, and supporting the individual member and collective membership for the flexible, collaborative organization; (4) sustaining personal energy level while maintaining a balance between work and outside responsibilities; (5) maintaining presence; and (6) establishing an environment of trust.

Competencies

Leadership competencies are often cumulative, requiring that leaders learn task and relationship skills on their feet over time. The soft skills of flexibility and adaptability are often a result of successful performance competencies. When someone is feeling successful, growth-fostering relational interactions multiply; success breeds success. Spirals of performance indicate whether the member is successful (upward spiral) or unsuccessful (downward spiral) and create impressions of competence or incompetence. These impressions lead to respect or disrespect, affecting the amount of open, enthusiastic support offered by co-members.

Past, Present, and Future Organizational Strategies

An organization has a strategy that defines what business it is in or wants to be in and the kind of organization it is or wants to be (Robbins, 1993). Most organizations (and their members) would prefer to control their own destiny. In order to do so, they design strategies to affect the environments in which they are attempting to succeed, striving to eliminate uncertainties; they base decisioning for the future on the successes of the past and the innovations and beneficial actualities of the present. The goal is to positively influence what is happening in the whole system now to create a better future.

Successful leadership means holding the system to processes that will nurture and sustain awareness of the organization's potential. Relational strategies deal with issues, opportunities, and roadblocks to the vision of the future in ways that do not disconnect members from what has worked well in the past but rather use those positive experiences as a basis for future achievement (Hammond, 1996).

Hiring, Sponsoring, and Supporting Members

Setting standards for who is hired with what skills and characteristics is a bottom-lines issue. The leader's ability to hire effective co-members may depend on that leader's assumptions regarding the needs of the organization. Hiring the wrong person with the right competencies or the right person with the wrong competencies can affect the organization's decisioning, whether the hiree is CEO or secretary. However, hiring co-members who do not fit may be a benefit to the organization in some cases: These persons can bring in new ideas and new ways of looking at things.

Hiring, with today's legalities of firing, is a big responsibility (and often a crapshoot). Keeping top performers is even more important. Sponsorship and support are significant to retaining top-performing members, to their acceptance by co-members, and to their performance on the job (see Chapter Seven).

Energy

Because of the high emotional and physical demands placed on them, relational leaders may initiate actions and activities that are confusing for co-members. Even the most enthusiastic, driven leader is occasionally overwhelmed by these demands, which may lead to flagging energy levels and decreased ability to cope. Members consider observed energy level to be representative of the leader's commitment to the causes he or she is promoting. To keep members from noticing a decline in energy, leader-members spend extra time responding to members' needs. Thus the leader is stretched thin, not having the time to concentrate on other demanding accountabilities. The result is a leader who is working long hours, not attending to his or her health needs, and feeling pressured to do more in less time. Achieving balance in time and energy while sustaining connections with members may be one of the biggest challenges for the relational leader-member, especially during times of organizational turbulence.

Presence

People both inside and outside the workplace are watching. What the leader says and does, the responses he or she gives verbally and nonverbally, are to the observers an indication of the authenticity of the leader. Is it important to be perfect? Or, rather, is it important to be authentic, thus creating and sustaining relationships that are realistic and relational? For a leader to strive for a perfect presence is to eventually disconnect and fail as a leader. Being "perfect" delivers the message that no help is needed or wanted: I can do this alone (exclusive independence). To strive for honest and open connections, while encouraging those who are self-consciously trying out leadership by challenging the status quo and delivering tentative messages, is authentic presence.

Some would say that poise (as in being dignified and collected) is important to presence. In an informal workplace in which people talk about the Pittsburgh Steelers, one cannot always be poised. It is neither necessary nor desirable to get down and dirty, or to be inappropriate, but it is beneficial to understand what presence means to the members—what they see and understand as authentic. They want a leader who is genuinely interested in, concerned about, and appreciative of what they do every day to contribute to the well-being of the organization. Being dignified won't always do it; being authentic will.

To have presence means to be authentic, genuine, reliable, and trustworthy. It also means that the leader has an accepting stance, and is nonjudgmental and open to differences. It means indirectly delivering the message to co-members that, as Meg Wheatley (1996) says, "The greatest gift we can tell you is that you are not alone."

Trust

Members come to trust leaders over time based on observations and perceptions. Is this person reliable and consistent? Someone we can respect? Open and honest? It is a challenge to gain and retain the trust of members who have been let down by previous leaders and it adds to the complexities of being a relational leader. A leader needs trust (based on consistency, reliability, openness, and honesty) and respect to be credible.

The leader relies on the advocacy gestures of those who report directly to him or her to gain the trust and commitment of the overall membership. When these people demonstrate trust and strong connections and promote the leader as credible, belief spreads across the organization. Conversely, when a direct report makes disparaging remarks about the leader, co-members and customers listen closely. If the messenger seems credible, listeners will decide the information is probably true. If the messenger is not credible, they will decide to check out the information. Even if the information is later discounted, it is not totally forgotten; it will always be there to be reconsidered: Where there is smoke, there must be fire. Formal or informal leaders, wherever they are in the organization, can destroy potential acceptance of a new leader with a few careless remarks.

Bottom-Lines Complexities

The leader's role is to keep the organization focused on staying viable in the marketplace. The leader's relational connections are important to exceptional decisioning. Leaders seek input in making decisions to expand, retract, redirect, and redesign organizations for survival and growth. Leader-members indirectly "decide" the depth and validity of the decisioning information they receive by making it possible, even comfortable, for co-members to deliver bottom-line bad news. The leader who experiences being on the receiving end of a messenger's willingness to challenge what is happening is successfully leading.

Relational leaders use quantitative and qualitative measurements for reaching the best long-term decisions. They may sacrifice profitable short-term solutions for long-term benefit regarding the three bottom lines. Through cross-organizational partnerships, members participate in the design and implementation of community visions of the future regarding human, ethical, and financial outcomes. It is through participating in these activities that future leaders emerge.

Visiting Leaders

Today we have "transitioning leaders"—leaders at the top who are visitors, expecting to contribute significantly and then leave. I once worked with a leader who was summoned from a meeting to the phone—never to return to the meeting or the organization. Within one hour, he was gone to a promotion position, calling back with transitional messages for his interim successor. When there is transition in leadership, members are shaken and concerned about the new leader, what that person's agenda will be, how each member will fit into the new leader's management mode. Productivity falters, members gossip, feelings of loss and insecurity set in. Of course, in some cases, when a bad leader moves on, excitement prevails and hope returns.

In large companies, the members at the edges may not feel significantly affected by the change in top leadership—at least not immediately. In smaller companies, members are in closer contact and more aware when change at the top occurs. But large or small, the old way—in which one person runs the show—is detrimental in a transitioning leader organization. Each time the leader moves on, there is disruption and discontinuity, verifying the need for many across the circle to be involved in decisioning. More people will be aware of how things are done and why, a necessity for maintaining the decisioning processes of the organization during the learning process of the new leader.

Learning

When leaders enter or are promoted within an organization, they bring with them a résumé of experience and accomplishment that has leveraged them into a new position of accountability. Unfortunately, past experience does not always prepare the new leader for what is ahead: There will be a learning period, and the opportunity to succeed often hinges on the new leader's ability to work with and lead with in new, unfamiliar territory. The competencies of the relational leader are built around learning.

Learning, as an ongoing process, requires us to be adaptable and resilient while continuing to grow and accumulate knowledge in chaotic environments. Learning often involves connecting and interacting with others, on and off the job. Learning is achieved through three qualities that are relational interactions. These interactions expand all members' abilities to grasp the concepts of the Principles of Membership and are especially significant to the concepts of leadership. These qualities are:

1. *Interdependence.* Members work together. Interdependence involves the willingness to contribute to the success and growth of others and the understanding that these opportunities make it possible for both parties to benefit.
2. *Mutuality.* Each participant expects to grow through the relationship and is willing to be an expert, an observer, and a learner at the appropriate times.
3. *Reciprocity.* Both parties have opportunities to be teacher and learner as needed in relational interactions of learning.

Coming into the organization from the outside, the new leader may be wearing rose-colored glasses; assumptions of the organizational past, present, and future may or may not match reality. Arriving with them on is one thing; keeping them on is another. Understanding the true picture can be arduous, requiring commitments of patience, perseverance, and time. When there is a lot to accomplish, these qualities may be in short supply for the new leader. But moving ahead based on assumptions can be detrimental to the success of the leader and his or her new organization. If the members have previously worked under a feared and mistrusted leader, it will take time for the leader to gain open input from individuals and the group, so needed linkages may be difficult to achieve. The actions and responses of the new leader's direct reports will affect present and future organizational strategies. "Fancy footwork" (Argyris, 1990) increases when these members are jockeying for position, attempting to look authoritative, subtly testing the new boss, covering up problems until the "right time" for disclosure, pointing the leader in the favored direction, and causing uncertainty until they find out what makes the new leader tick. The trick for them is to find out how to act and respond to the new leader in order to keep their jobs and gain favor. The ability of the new leader to pull the group together as a contributing membership group will affect future strategies of the organization.

New but experienced leaders are often recruited to bring improvement and change to organizations—change that is not always obvious to organizational members. Mort Meyerson (1997), in an article in *Fast Company*, told about leaving EDS proud of the company, its people, and its accomplishments during his seven years with the organization. It had been unbelievably successful. After he left he had second thoughts. "What I realized after I left was that I had also made a lot of people very unhappy. Our people paid a high price for their economic success. Eighty-hour weeks were the norm. . . . We asked people to put financial performance above everything else, and they did . . . even if it meant too much personal sacrifice or doing things that weren't really in the best interests of customers" (p. 6).

In 1992, Meyerson was recruited by Ross Perot to move to Perot Systems as CEO. After six months, he was concerned. It looked like the same mistake was going to be repeated. Intentional change had to happen—with his own style of leading and with the organization and the way it worked with its customers. His reasoning was clear: "In a world where the lines between companies, industries, and even nations get blurred, a leader builds an effective organization around values and work style. And a leader learns to define success in business as both producing financial strength and generating a team of people who support and nurture each other" (p. 10).

Change Agent

The ability to perform successfully as an agent for change is significant to the role of formal and informal leadership. As noted previously, all members lead. In the hierarchical, bureaucratic organization, the level of the members initiating change is more important than it is in the Membership Organization. All members across the circle see needs and are frustrated unless they can address those needs. All members are significant to achieving change and to the success of change initiatives. The ability of the change agent to influence in times of change is relevant to the leader's ability to lead relationally.

The term *change agent* is defined as someone (or something) that initiates a change or shift in a given situation or circumstance. If a change effort is anticipated, someone has to manage or facilitate the change process—another "working with" linking role. The ideal change agent is internal to the organization and can be at the formal leader-member level or on the production floor. Wherever he or she is in the organization, an internal change agent often faces the risk that others may see him or her as "singing out of tune" with what is acceptable at the moment. Change agents will be vulnerable to the whims of both organizational leader-members and co-members.

For this reason, change agents need resilience, persistence, support, money, authority, experience, protection, and acceptance by leader-members; they need the ability to listen, influence, partner, connect, and effectively suppress their own ego. They also need direct sponsorship, authority, and appropriate partnerships to serve as signs of legitimacy for what they are attempting to accomplish, proportionate to the size of the change being initiated. They also may require forgiveness; change agents may seem unreasonable and unrealistic because they

- See a different reality
- Speak the unspeakable
- Challenge the status quo
- Anticipate the future
- Initially are seen as less than credible

Co-members often see change agents as being trouble. In status quo organizations, even the leader may say to slow down, keep out of the way, or forget it and leave things as they are— change will upset people. In such an organization, introducing new ways of marketing, new customer service programs, or new "soft" training may even put the change agent at risk—especially if the change agent is a new or nontraditional person in the group. Change agents tend to be innovators and suggesters of the outrageous. They may be unusually curious or may happen to see something significant. Some will say that the change agent likes the excitement of seeking, achieving change, and going against the norm. In some cases, this may be true, but many times the agent is the normal, everyday member who sees a need and feels strongly enough about it to follow it through. It should also be noted that change agents may not necessarily see themselves as such. Unfortunately, many times change agents are faced with convincing the unconvinced because what they see is not seen by others. The first challenge of the change agent is to enroll others.

Delivering Hope

Accomplishing change often depends on the ability of the agent for change to deliver hope and the willingness of organizations to tolerate the existence of change agents within the organization. Many organizations are stagnating, struggling, and/or on the verge of demise. Their members are fearful, angry, and waiting for the other shoe to drop. Active, successful change agents may be the only hope for returning such organizations to being profitable and energized. Yet these change agents are often ignored, chastised, and even fired. Even in the final struggle for survival, some organizations will ignore the pleas of their internal change agents to "just listen, really listen, just once."

To actively seek and initiate change in an organization, department, or group that values the status quo or stability can be a painful undertaking. Although the change agent may consider the struggle to be a challenge, other members, tied to the past, may see the agent as creating problems, causing disturbances, or wanting to change things that don't need to be changed. The responses will vary from resistance, to indifference, to resignation, to enthusiasm—all of which can change or revert quickly and unexpectedly. Geoffrey Bellman (1992), when discussing the change agent, says,

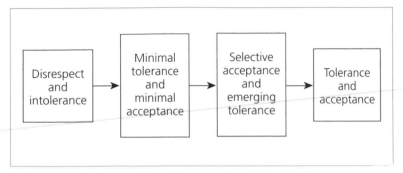

FIGURE 4   Change Entrance Sequence

When they see you coming down the hall, their hearts will not always beat with anticipation of the wonderful new ideas you are bringing them! Because of their emphasis on predictability and stability, they can easily move to defensive posture. . . . The change opportunities you bring to your internal customers are often seen as threats to the procedures they have established. (p. 6)

An organization that does not have active change agents throughout the circle will lose hope, stagnate, and eventually die. The writer George Bernard Shaw once said that all progress depends on the unreasonable man (or woman) (Handy, 1989). *Unreasonable* in this case means someone willing to change things and address "know to do" and "how to do" issues of change—and initiate and shift things to the way he or she thinks is more reasonable. The change agent tends to take the phrase "we are the organization" very seriously. For this reason, the change agent is willing, at least in the beginning, to work on the fringes of tolerance and acceptance.

Tolerating Change

General co-member response to a change agent's suggestions varies according to the way the agent introduces the change and the way the receiver of the change responds. The entry point of the member is indicative of the amount of resistance, information, participation, and support the change will receive from the member or group to whom the change is being proposed (see Figure 4).

If the proposed change is perceived as a major shift and feels threatening, the member(s) may enter the change sequence at the *disrespect and intolerance* point. This entrance signals caution for the change agent; this group may actively seek to form a strong counterculture that may resist and derail any possibilities of success for the change. Heels are dug in. Sabotage may occur.

When a member or group enters at the *minimal tolerance and minimal acceptance* point, resistance is their priority. They may see the change as inevitable and try to slow its pace, dragging their feet, showing visible discomfort, and reluctantly waiting to see how things go. This group may eventually join the more indignant group if the latter group (or an influential informal leader) pressures them.

Members entering at *selective acceptance and emerging tolerance* include those who see the change as being potentially beneficial or believe that pieces of the change may work but are reluctant and not completely convinced. These individuals may be looking for ways to accept what is happening; they will see some of the changes as important. They may openly attempt to influence and strike bargains regarding the amount of change being proposed. If convinced, this group could prove to be a good resource for the effective change agent.

Those entering at early *tolerance and acceptance* of the proposed changes willingly seek and offer information and support. Open involvement and early buy-in allows this group to quickly reach a level of comfort with the proposal. This group may aid in convincing other group or organizational members of the benefits of the pending change.

Accepting Discomfort

The ability of change agents to be persistent, to hang in there during the change process, may depend on their responses to interactions during the change process. It is a rare person who does not experience discomfort while serving as a change agent. There may be both obvious and hidden risks that cause the agent to be constantly alert, and there may be pressure from others to perform, creating a sense of urgency. It is important for an agent to accept the realities of the role in order to survive. To do so requires the agent to seek leader support, take steps to align others, and accept that discomfort is inevitable.

Gaining the input and acceptance of the group, knowing what has to be done, having the financial backing and support of the organizational leaders, and maintaining a level of resilience helps the change agent cope with discomfort. But there will still be bumpy roads ahead with unforeseen problems and miscommunications that disrupt the process. Accepting discomfort and remaining resilient require change agents to

- Have a strong belief in their own capabilities and in what is being done
- Have high energy and strong financial backing
- Give others the benefit of the doubt
- Always do more than is expected
- Assume that everything that happens is a learning event
- Know that working with/leading with will make change possible
- Have a faith that never fails

The activities of the individual change agent working in a normal, everyday job require the willingness to risk new ways of doing things. An ability to work with and deal with the powers-that-be as well as reluctant, keep-it-the-same co-members is also essential. To think that change agents exist only when big changes are to be made is discounting the enthusiasm and energy members put into identifying how to do their work better each day. Individual acts of identifying what is economically worth changing, discovering how to do it, and then going for it can make a difference both in an organization's ability to achieve and in members' feelings of competence and significance, wherever they stand in the company.

Facing Difficulties

In Membership Organizations, leaders understand that when bad things happen, all members are stressed, suspicious, and vulnerable. Members who have previously felt secure and safe respond with fear and concern. Active members become passive, and previously positive, innovative contributors step back to "working safe," taking fewer risks and asking fewer questions. Members do not like surprises. Open, informative discussions solicit understanding and involvement. Withholding truth ultimately destroys change agent credibility.

The need for change is inevitable, and the role of the successful relational leader is to examine, recognize, acknowledge, support, and connect the membership to the need for change. When necessary, the leader-member leads down the path of reluctance and resistance, pulling and encouraging members along. If the leader has proven trustworthy, credible, and open, that makes it possible for members to remain enrol-led while the change process unfolds. Dictating, manipulating, politicizing, and banging members over the head won't work.

In the Membership Organization, members know when change is needed because they are deeply involved in organizational realities. Change may be initiated by members anywhere in the organization; as influencing agents, they see trends not seeable from where the leader sits, and they create partnerships and linkages with formal leaders and informal leaders to achieve those changes.

Summary

In the past, leadership was seen as a means of "winning the prize." Leaders were bold, brave, and commanding, leading breathless, conflicted, exhausted managers who did as they were told. Organizations accepted this as the way things were done and the way to beat the competition. Although leaders who are willing to take on the tough stuff are vital to organizational success, being abusive and detached no longer is acceptable—or profitable.

Sustainability requires that members be treated as contributing adults, able to make decisions beneficial to the organization. How others see them (whether or not as capable and contributing members) has an impact on their actions and responses in the workplace. The style of leading and the worldview of leader-members affect what is done and what is said about the organization by the members and the customers. New methods for succeeding as co-members throughout the circle, whether performing a leadership task or performing as an expert in what we do every day, are creating a new kind of workplace community. Eventually the new relational community will be understood as the way to achieve top performance both individually and in the workplace community.

7

Many employees misunderstand the social contract between employer and employee, believing that as long as they go on showing up for work, the company will go on rewarding their "loyalty" with lifetime employment. . . . *The truth is, no company can afford to keep employees who fail to create enough value for customers to more than cover their own compensation.* [Emphasis added.]

Frederick F. Reichheld,
The Loyalty Effect

PRINCIPLE 6

Accountability

> Members are willingly and
> individually responsible and
> accountable for working
> toward organizational
> goals.

We have all worked with people who do little other than try to look busy and bother other people. What work they attempt is done in a slipshod manner. These people are the reason for the word *entitled* as used in the workplace. Their ability to work hard all day without actually doing anything does not go unnoticed. Many years ago, I worked in a large industrial facility and was frantically busy all day every day, many weekends and holidays, too. But each day I would see the same people being mediocre. Everyone saw it, and everyone watched management ignore it. The "coffee walkers," for example, spent most of the day drinking coffee, walking their cups from office to office, from machine to machine. Yet many of them took home a larger paycheck than most of the observers and received cost-of-living bonuses and raises at the same time the observers did. The organization was perpetuating mediocrity.

But things changed at this organization when success became elusive. Many of the coffee walkers are still working there—but now they are *working*. The organization convinced them it would not allow them to retire while still coming to work every day. Presumably management said, "Produce or someone else will," or, better yet, "In order for this company to succeed, we need your input," then actively sought, required, acted on, and acknowledged their input. The organization made some big changes that worked. The members are now taking responsibility for the organization's success.

Responsibility in this context is perceived as an internal choice regarding the amount of energy to be used in fulfilling accountabilities, which are external nonchoice performance expectations.

Responsibility

In the past, being responsible meant members were doing what they were expected to do, when they were expected to do it, and how they were expected to do it. In most cases, it allowed some members to underfunction and others to overfunction. To be responsible was to participate in working relationships only to the level expected by the person delegating the work, no more, no less. When change occurred in their shared "contract" for performance, both the underfunctioning member and the overfunctioning member would attempt to restore the previous relationship (Lerner, 1985). All members worked at maintaining the status quo in workplace relationships.

In the Membership Organization, deep participation places the accountability for top performance with all members of the workplace community. Unfortunately, when the organization increases the accountability of the underfunctioning individual or group, participants may become alarmed. Underfunctioning was comfortable and undemanding or at least it was the known way, and it worked to some degree. Creating a more level working community is scary: Who knows how it will really work or even if it will work?

For members to feel significant, each individual must become a top performer, overfunctioning in the workplace community. In order for this to happen, the organization must challenge the concept of lack of individual responsibility. If underfunctioning members are to participate in the new workplace community, their definitions of responsibility must be changed.

To be a willingly responsible person requires the individual member to make a self-empowering decision regarding personal level of contribution. In an organization that is inviting deep participation by the membership, each person, with the support of co-members, can move beyond underfunctioning to willing responsibility and accountability, becoming a functional contributor. Self-monitoring increases, initiating new and risky actions of responsibility.

It is difficult to erase personally generated past performance limitations. All participants must be willing to forgive. An organizational community that takes steps toward empowerment and top performance must be forgiving while inviting increased choices of responsibility. This makes it possible for the individual (and the collective membership) to become more productive and innovative while working in a positive atmosphere.

Responsibility as Emotional

Choosing to increase one's responsibility is an emotional act. Willing responsibility requires members to set aside magnified issues of the past that are blocking deep participation and their ability to be top performers. This is not to discount feelings of helplessness and hopelessness left over from the controlling and disruptive management structures of the past. Those feelings are real and hard to set aside. To do so requires that all members move toward inclusion, acceptance, and participation.

But some members focus on the negative and ignore the positive (and there always is positive) that makes it possible to move to connected partnerships. Allcorn (1994) states, "Some people readily overpersonalize events, overgeneralize, and pay selective attention to only those aspects of life experience that tend to reinforce their suspicious and paranoid views of the world" (p. 37). Such members seek negative, win-lose activities to justify and reinforce feelings of entitlement and criticality. Reinforcement includes expressing anger, being competitive, seeking perfection, and avoiding involvement.

Anger
Anger is a burst of strong, emotional arousal that is caused by resentment, injustice, or displeasure, potentially leading to a

desire to retaliate. In most cases, anger is short term; it is dealt with and then subsides. When the member is frustrated and prevented from expressing the anger, it may remain hidden but erupt later.

Unfortunately, anger, hidden or not, begets anger. If it is not resolved, there is a tendency to return to the angry state over and over again, decreasing the ability of those involved to deal with the frustrations of the "anger-producing" relationship (McKay, Rogers, & McKay, 1989). Rigidity, intolerance, inflexibility, helplessness, and hopelessness increase steadily, and constructive performance diminishes. Defensiveness increases, connections dissolve.

Carol Tavris (1989) says that "anger is the human hiss" (p. 47). Anger is a cry for help, indicating to others that something is wrong, undesirable, that there are barriers, feelings of insignificance. Anger means that something needs attention. It is important for leader-members to listen well, ask questions, and dig for the reason for the anger. Anger tends to escalate and perpetuate the root issue (which is not necessarily the issue causing the explosion at hand). Listening for what the member is really saying and addressing the real message can be an effective anger-avoidance technique. Jack Miller, president of Quill Corporation in Lincolnville, Illinois, says, "You have to take the time to listen extra hard. People don't always speak out or speak directly to what they really want to say. In my role as a leader, I can miss a lot when I charge ahead without listening. I am constantly reminding myself to stop and listen with more than just my ears. I have to tune my 'senses' to hear what they really want to say. It makes a big difference in what I really hear."

But anger can also be constructive. Allcorn (1994) states, "The constructive expression of anger leads to creativity, risk taking, and industrious work" (p. 107). In this context, the angry person makes a responsible choice by turning anger into a productive stimulus. Anger can be constructive if the member so chooses.

Competition

Reinforcement through competition refers to members' desire for achievement at any cost. These members (1) sense that co-members will not support them in achieving their goals;

(2) often demonstrate impatience, hostility, and high levels of ambition; and (3) are usually driven by the need to look good in the eyes of the powers that be.

Their sense that others will not support them leads them to be demanding, manipulative, and controlling. Competitors believe their co-members may get in their way or must be forced to support their cause. They push themselves and others, sometimes dictating what must be done, when, and how. Competitors are not relational members. Relationships are problems, not benefits, in their quest to achieve. Such people are not fun to work with, if indeed it is possible to really work with them.

The heavily competitive person will be exclusively independent on the Personal Mastery Continuum (see Chapter Two), preferring to work on their own so they do not have to share the glory. Yet when working in a team, they will remind others, "Hey, we're a team here, remember?" when things aren't going their way. They are really good at guilt tripping others on the team when forced to do things in ways not explicitly to their advantage.

Because of their competitiveness, they are often adept at getting education and training and grabbing control of areas in which they can be the only expert. They withhold information, parceling it out only when needed, and do not train others (for fear that they may surpass them in expertise), all of which keeps them in the role of the sole expert.

The hierarchical, bureaucratic structures of the past encouraged political campaigning in order to make it into the inner circle. The competitive person often campaigns. Competitors need to win, be first, or be recognized by the people who count. Their methods of attaining recognition by "the leaders" ostracize and separate them from co-members, who are leery of them because of their tendency to push others aside, use them, even jeopardize their co-members' careers in their quest to achieve their own goals. Their tendency to perform when those to be impressed are around and then to drop their act when they are not is often obvious to their co-members, causing distrust.

Perfectionism

Perfectionists seek reinforcement through striving for perfection for themselves, their group, and their organization. Setting standards of performance that are excessively high, driving themselves and others to achieve them, and then being upset when those goals are not met are actions typical of perfectionists. Their message is that "perfect" is possible if only (something) were done right.

Perfectionists think that detail and order, rigid adherence to standards, being in control, and being overly careful can result in perfection. As leader-members, they micromanage their subordinates, demand more information, instruct those who already know how, and analyze, analyze, analyze. Of course, their ability to lead is limited: If members rush the other way when they see the perfectionist down the hall, there is no one to lead. Not surprisingly, such leaders have a superiority complex: I am the only one who really knows how to do your work; I am criticizing you to make you better; I am the only one who is right; If you are committed enough, your work will be perfect; and so on. The superiority complex requires that there be inferior persons in the exchange, and perfectionists make it clear who is inferior. They need to reinforce their belief in the deficits of others.

Problems also abound with perfectionist members: They struggle in group relationships because they are never satisfied with the work of others; they may appear to procrastinate because there is never enough information to complete a task; they may spend inappropriate amounts of time on low-priority tasks, unable to desert any task, no matter the priority, to go on to another unless it is completed to their satisfaction; they may bother people by seeking excessive guidance on how to do something perfectly the first time.

These members also believe there is certainty where none exists. In their passion for control, they believe there is one answer (theirs), and thus they eliminate the questions of co-members. In today's complex working communities, perfectionists will struggle with any reality that cannot be dealt with through linear thinking or that forces them to seek input from partnerships across the circle. Their partnerships are thus few and short lived.

Avoidance

Seeking to maintain the status quo is a reinforcement technique. The past was always perfect; change is always wrong; staying the same is always more comfortable. The Principles of Membership create new responsibilities, accountabilities, and deeper participation, initially generating for members a sense of being out of control. That feeling is threatening and uncomfortable for the person seeking reinforcement; avoidance is the first response.

Avoiding actions occur when there is insecurity. For the person seeking security, the new way of working will be scary. For others, the newfound freedom of decisioning that accompanies deeper participation creates a sense of excitement—with new fears regarding the "what ifs" of making those decisions. If one steps away from the route well traveled, the sense of direction rapidly erodes. Avoiding decisioning in the past eliminated responsibility and accountability. When responsibility and accountability become personal, avoidance will not go unnoticed.

The Law of Responsibility

Members add value to organizations by proactively applying the law of responsibility: The individual makes a choice about how to do the work and what attitude to have toward that work and the workplace community. That attitude—whether it be enrollment, disinterest, or rebellion—is reflected in the responses and level of participation displayed by the member. The word *no* used to be the safest word in the workplace: No, that's not the way it's done around here; no, that's not my job; no, don't listen to them; no, I don't want to do that; no, my idea's better. In the new workplace, members think before they say no. *Yes* is the first considered response, and every opportunity to perform is seen as an opportunity to perform well. The choice is to be a contributing, learning, employable member in the organization—or not to be a member.

Members make choices to sign on, get out, or rebel (Kouzes & Posner, 1993). Personal, individual decisions to take responsibility are consciously and unconsciously shared with others inside and outside of the community. What is said and done tells others what the individual thinks about co-members and about the organization. Those who point fingers, blame their organization, and stay on the job as value-less members have decided to rebel. The organizational environment does influence member responses—but the individual who decides to say no instead of discussing concerns has abdicated his or her own ability to influence. Responses can range from not performing at all (the "no"), to doing just enough to make it look like something has been done (mediocrity), to doing it in a consultative, collaborative, exemplary way.

Responsibility includes taking action that makes a difference. Actions of the individual members are significant to the bottom-lines achievement of their organization. If members' actions do not make a difference, they are not employable. No matter where members are in the organizational circle, their first responsibility to the organization (and themselves) is to apply themselves to their work. Their value-added actions justify payment for their work investment. If actions do not justify a paycheck, the member is valueless to co-members and to the organization. In these times, the organization that retains valueless members is allowing those members to negatively influence one or all three bottom lines.

Being responsible means getting rid of the victim mentality. A popular response is to blame "them." The member says "they" are unreasonable; "they" make things difficult because they don't care; "they" don't know what they are doing. Management says "they" just don't care about doing good work anymore; "they" do as little as possible; "they" are never around when needed. "They" are whatever group the victims resent.

Victims whine and complain—to the wrong people. They tend to be intolerant, apathetic, and respectful of only a few. They are passive and in general let life happen *to them* rather than the other way around. They are hard people to admire. They have somehow learned to succeed in chosen segments of their life by being victims. (Their idea of success is surely different from that of the value-added member.)

Because they are usually mediocre performers, victims are good at making excuses. There is always a reason why someone else should be blamed for their own lack of performance. Gerard Egan (1990) describes four categories of excuses:

1. *Complacency:* Failure to see the seriousness of the situation ("If someone had told me, I would have done it better")

2. *Rationalization:* Clinging to bad assumptions or distorted information ("It was never that important before")
3. *Procrastination:* Putting off, exploring problems endlessly, waiting ("Need more information" or "Don't have to do it right now")
4. *Passing the buck:* Waiting for someone else to "fix it" ("That's not my job" or "They were supposed to . . . ")

Making excuses is a way of life for these members—and they believe their excuses are valid. Excuse making perpetuates their victim mentality, but it also creates barriers to achieving credibility in their work group. It soon becomes obvious that victims cannot be relied upon to do their share or to do it well.

To get rid of the victim mentality, the victim must look for what he or she can do to make things better. In many organizations, being positive can be a real challenge, but we each have to take that challenge. Each member is responsible for deciding to get rid of his or her own victim mentality. Each member has competencies to bring to the workplace that can make a difference, or else a mistake was made when he or she was hired. Being responsible and being a victim do not mix.

The victim complex is catching: One bad apple spoils the barrel. If victimization starts in an organization and is reinforced as appropriate behavior, it will spread. This is based on the principle that one way to determine what is correct is by looking around to see what others do. If uniqueness and individuality are discouraged and being a victim is accepted, people think it must be appropriate behavior, and they copy it.

Being a responsible member also includes the willingness to change. I-know-and-accept-that-I-am-the-only-one-I-can-change also means that an individual can change if the need is there. A member cannot motivate anyone but himself or herself to change but can provide information, encouragement, and tolerance when others face difficult times.

The workplace can be a nightmare or an adventure—or in all likelihood somewhere in between. When members face the fact that each person can make a difference and act on that realization, things happen. As discussed in Chapter Two, it is important for each person to recognize that when one person changes, things around that person change. Each person can and should be a catalyst, not a saboteur.

Thus being responsible suggests that organizational members individually and when performing in responsible partnerships can make things work. The resulting feelings of urgency regarding the organization's goals and overall performance generate top performance for the members and the workplace community.

Accountability

In the past, accountability was limited to a process of evaluation used to gain improvement, find out who did something, or determine why that particular thing was done. When a member was held accountable, it was probably painful, was usually performed by those in power, and was an insinuation that there was a problem that someone needed to own up to. In such an organization, accountability was either nonexistent or was foisted upon only those who were out of favor. When accountability was assigned, it was held out as an example for all to see. The message was, Take notice and don't do this.

In one chain store, a cashier was "put on accountability" because she had taken too long with a transaction with a customer and the attention of the floor supervisor was flagged. When asked by a co-worker what "accountability" meant, she responded that she was to attend additional training and that her performance would be more closely scrutinized for a certain length of time "even if the problem was not her fault."

In call centers, technology tracks response times, number of calls, and length of conversations, indirectly encouraging short conversations that may not fully meet the customers' needs. In a Membership Organization, this is rarely seen as accountability. The member who is rewarded for the number of customer contacts separates the experience from an experience of accountability.

In the Membership Organization, productive, hard-working members *prefer* to be held accountable when accountability is tied to respect and dignity of the individual and rewards are distributed honestly and appropriately. After all, one can only be held accountable if one is capable.

Bardwick (1991) notes, "People prefer accountability; they want to be rewarded when they work hard and they want those who don't to be punished. They want their work to be judged because it is the only way to feel that their work is significant" (p. 51). Being accountable is one of the ways members earn the right to be right and the right to be wrong. Members learn and grow through accountability and offer the same opportunity to others. When linked to learning how to become a top performer, accountability is a tool for increasing member competency, empowerment, challenge, and significance.

Researchers have found that accountability is a "binding quality" of organizational life, without which organizational life would be increasingly precarious and tentative. Accountability provides an important vision of behavioral expectations within the organization (Cummings & Anton, 1990). As a mechanism for exchange, accountability can stimulate opportunities for productive, consultative conversations or, when performed to "straighten a person out," can be used to defame, degrade, and destroy partnerships. (Accountability events are judged as fair or unfair, appropriate or inappropriate, by all parties involved.)

In the Membership Organization, where members do not work in isolation, positive partnerships create new visions of how work is done and by whom. Members now work together across the organizational circle, requiring new frameworks for accountability, a new language of benefit and effectiveness. Three assumptions define accountabilities: (1) being accountable for, (2) being accountable to, and (3) to whom the accountabilities are distributed.

Being Accountable For

Being accountable for identifies what must be done to succeed. Members are hired to perform assigned, dedicated activities based on an implied or existing job description. These assignments are to be performed by a specific member or group, who have a duty to perform the assigned task.

These assigned accountabilities include standards of performance based on past success. *Being accountable for* assumes that the member is capable of performing the assigned task or will be trained to do so.

Being Accountable To

Being accountable to someone or to a group is essential to achievement in the workplace. The need for checks and balances is human. Even the signers of the Constitution understood the implications of not initiating accountability. Of course, it is the strength of the act of accountability that affects the equilibrium of a relationship and its significance to performance.

Accountability is influenced by the amount of responsibility the member has chosen to put into performance. In organizations, the motivation to perform is an outcome of the consequences of "doing." Members ask themselves, If I do this, how will others react?, thus automatically making it necessary to construct acceptable accounts of what is being done (Tetlock, 1990). With a boss who requires too much accountability, the member is wary about how the boss will react, which may lower the willingness of the member to empower him- or herself to achieve the best possible results.

Humans, being naturally self-centered, seek balance in constructive accountability. This implies that the opposite of accountability, lack of accountability, is problematic also. The underzealous leader delivers the message that it really doesn't matter if members go the extra mile to achieve top performance, whereas the overzealous leader, who is always watching and controlling, decreases the members' desire to perform.

Overzealousness increases anxiety, erodes feelings of safety, and undermines the member's self-respect. Underzealous leader-members may cause feelings of abandonment, loss of hope, and detachment. These extremes induce coping strategies to combat feelings of anxiety caused by attempts to meet the leaders' expectations. Leaders who practice extremes do not create an environment in which real empowerment and deep participation are seen as possible or safe.

Distribution of Accountabilities

In the Membership Organization, decisioning opportunities and accountabilities are spread across the organization to the members closer to the location of the decision, as discussed in Chapter Three. Members throughout the organization are empowered to be active decisioning agents. Accountability for performance of the overall organization is thus spread to the edges of the circle. All members are now expected to be consultative (thinking) and performing (doing) members of the organization. Each contributes, accepting increased personal responsibility for how things work.

When accountability is distributed across the organization by the use of cross-circle teams, awareness and knowledge are tapped, increasing decisioning activities at the place the decision is most beneficial. In the past, engineers were accountable to make decisions the floor persons heard about only when implemented—when their feedback might result in costly adjustments to the product. Cross-circle teams design and implement programs that involve in the decisioning process representatives of all possible constituencies—including customers. By using cross-circle teams, accountability is spread throughout the circle. Members being affected are able to participate—it is part of their assigned role to affect the positive performance of their department. Participation increases the availability of the resources to perform, increases performance potential, and increases the pride and enrollment of the members—all because they were given the opportunity to be accountable for the participatory activity. Miscalculations and misuse of time and money are avoided. Accountability has been shared productively.

Accountability for, accountability to, and distributed accountability establish the need for members at all levels to create beneficial partnerships, as shown in Chapter Three. Accountability is no longer a one-way discussion. The right of all members to challenge in the right way is a confirmation of distributed accountability; there are now opportunities for all members to ask questions, get explanations, and expand their accountability.

Authority

A member may or may not have authority or power to decide or act on a decision. But not having the authority to get to the finish line on a task does not mean being excused from performance. An unauthorized member must find someone who does have the necessary authority. If, for example, the member is accountable for purchasing a new telephone system for $500,000 but is not able to approve the financial investment, then that member must find a partner with the authority to sign the contract for purchase—or else get the authority to do so. The partner may agree to sign or convince the member to delay purchase because of budgeting limitations (the partner's expert area)—their contribution toward completing the task. When authority is lacking, actively partnering with others to successfully complete assigned work is a membership activity.

In a healthy, productive, participative organization, where accountability and authority are distributed across the organization, members are willing to be accountable for their actions of authority. Top performers display high conviction in their work and are flexible and adaptable but stand by their decisioning. Accountability that is overly controlling disappears over time when members gain confidence and establish connections and partnerships that support their empowered actions of authority.

Implications of Authority and Accountability

Accountability and authority imply that the member has high *personal standards*. High (or low) personal standards are based on expertise and having the knowledge to perform. These standards are spread across the group when the member formally or informally serves as a knowledgeable and experienced informal peer trainer who is seen as credible, contributing, and effective.

Accountability and authority imply *liability*—being obligated or answerable for. When accountability and authority for organizational success are spread across the organization, the membership collectively assumes higher levels of significance in achieving organizational top performance. Personal pride in the outcomes and achievement of goals motivates members to re-enroll in their organization, as discussed in Chapter Three.

Accountability and authority imply that the member has *voice*. Researchers state that dysfunctional behavior is a result of accumulated emotions related to the experience of not being heard (Srivastva & Barrett, 1990). Voice, implying listening, valuing, and consideration of input, adds energy, connection, action, and the possibility of newly formed partnerships across the community.

Leader-members provide resources and opportunities for co-members to exercise responsibility, accountability, and authority. If members choose to be highly responsible, want to be successful in their accountability, and either have or seek needed authority, the next step for the leader-member is to get out of the way and support them in getting the job done—not do it for them. When responsibility, accountability, and authority are aligned (and the members are right for the accountability), members have the opportunity to do the best job they can. Micromanaging in an empowered membership environment does not work.

Mediocrity

Mediocre workers are neither consistently responsible nor generally accountable. The people with whom they work are usually unhappy with them because their work is not done well or pleasantly. They tell their external customers, if any, all about the bad things about their jobs, not the good things. The mediocre worker's internal customers regularly hear about the "too's" (see Chart 15). Of course, the organization also has "too's" about the mediocre member's performance.

In organizations in which working at mediocrity is ignored, polarities exist between the status levels. The less-thans and more-thans pretend "they" do not exist, knowing for sure that "us" is the only group contributing to the welfare of the

CHART 15 The Too's of the Mediocre Member	
The Mediocres Think the Organization Is	The Organization Thinks Mediocres Are
Too indifferent	Too indifferent
Too inflexible	Too inflexible
Too judgmental	Too negative
Too understaffed	Too underchallenged
Too demanding	Too unresponsive
Too slow	Too underworked
Too uncommunicative	Too status quo oriented
Too "stuck"	Too self-focused

organization. All are pointing fingers and not talking, figuratively standing back to back, telling everyone who will listen that nothing gets done around here because of "them."

Mediocre members practice self-protection. They may play the appearance game in an effort to bypass now-expected negative attention of supervisor and co-workers. For example, an army officer once described the way a recruit could survive without a lot of hassle: The trick was not to stand out among the other recruits, be "never in the front, never in the back, always in the middle." Similarly, the disinterested, mediocre, self-protective member never volunteers for extra work, never appears not to perform to minimum standard, hides in the crowd where no one will notice, uses "appearance of work" to stay uninvolved.

Playing the game of work through appearance in itself takes work. It includes always being alert to physical, control, contributing, knowledge, and team appearance, always being "there," not being the best, not being the worst, just getting along:

- *Physical appearance:* Work at fitting the group's perception of what a good group member looks like, encouraging the perception of you as fitting into the organization.
- *Control appearance:* Under all circumstances, act self-controlled, appropriate, and connected to the right people. Being out of control means being ostracized.

- *Personality appearance:* Appear friendly, self-assured, reasonable, and other focused. Just keep smiling.
- *Contributing appearance:* Always contribute to the well-being of the group and organization to the point of "acceptable." To do otherwise gets the attention of co-members.
- *Knowledge appearance:* Pretend at all costs that you know what you are doing, even if it is not true. In the learning organization, looking like you know counts.
- *Team appearance:* Go along with the group. Don't volunteer to take on tasks if decisions may be required—taking on potentially risky activities draws the attention of the group and you might do the wrong thing.

The likelihood that such members will choose to be responsible, accountable, or empowered is limited because they know that there is potential risk of higher expectations of performance. They do not want to be challenged; there is too much risk and potential for having to perform above mediocre. They just want to be there.

To assume accountability for their own work, members need to recognize, internalize and then act on the need for change. Members must see a reason to do it, accept that reason as valid, and then initiate self-change. And to change "self" requires the member to assume the role of self-leadership (Faren & Kaye, 1996). Even in the new world of teams, it is necessary for individuals to be accountable to themselves for their personal productivity. Self-accountability can be the toughest leader role the member has.

Positive Accountability

Membership, because of the voluntary implications of the term, suggests a strong desire by members to belong to and support their workplace community. Also, because of the characteristic of inclusiveness, there is an added dimension of "working with" in a more level working community. The Principles of Membership serve as a catalyst for and a component of high levels of internal responsibility and external accountability. As a result, there is a collective wisdom that sustains the perspective of accountability as a developmental, interactive opportunity for members across the organizational circle.

Accountability in the past produced frustration, histrionics, and complaints of unfairness. The process was to tell the member not to do that again and often did not provide the stimulus to keep on keeping on or allow for a "let's look at it together" approach. Appreciation and valuing was only reluctantly offered. The Membership Organization, as a relationship-based community, provides support, encouragement, and opportunities to perform as consultation partners in developmental accountability. The new language of responsibility and accountability includes positive dynamics of accountability that did not exist in the past.

Accountability includes *feedback and "feedforward"* (Shull, 1997). Feedback has been a part of the "evaluatory" aspect of organizations for a long time. But basing improvement on past performance does not actively open up the future to new possibilities of performance. Instead of looking at what was done wrong or right in the past, the member's questions should be, What should I do more of, what should I do less of, what should I stop, and what should I start, and what can we do to get them to make this possible? with an emphasis on how those five questions are tied to the topic under discussion. When there is a two-way feedforward conversation, both parties can assume the best about what can be accomplished in the future.

Finally, accountability means not being on a fault-finding mission. Accountability is seeking new understandings together and is used as a developmental tool for both (or all) members involved. Significant to achievement of constructive accountability is the membership concept of individual and mutual involvement in the success of our co-members and the organization. As noted by Srivastva and Barrett (1990), *"In the appreciative organization, all members from CEO to secretary take responsibility for the whole organization. All social activity is co-authored; members assume accountability for every organizational activity"* (p. 394; Srivasta and Barrett's italics).

Summary

The new language of responsibility (an internal act of identifying the desired level of energy to be applied) and accountability (an external assignment) sustains efforts to blur status and group boundaries in the Membership Organization. Top performance includes new levels of involvement and inclusion that stem from willing responsibility and accountability. All members, wherever they are in the workplace community, are responsible and accountable for the successful performance of their workplace community. As Peter Block (1995) says, "We need to keep one eye on the marketplace, for that is the ultimate focus of our accountability long term. But we cannot exercise accountability to the marketplace without also demonstrating internal accountability and answering our own questions about how we are living out our purpose" (p. 5). If members want their organizations to survive, they must participate, not only in performing their work but also in actively supporting change processes that will make it possible for their organizations, and they themselves, to achieve.

8

The leader of the future needs to provide active support to the critical cause of employee satisfaction and [enrollment]. . . . Employee contracts could be eliminated if employees trusted leadership to be their personal advocate. While the role of leader as servant has been cited as a new concept for management, we hope the role of leader as employee advocate will become a new management mind-set rather than just conceptual philosophy.

Susan Smith Kuczmarski and
Thomas D. Kuczmarski,
Values-Based Leadership

Advocacy

> Member willingness to
> promote co-members
> and the workplace
> community positively
> influences the performance
> of individuals, groups,
> and the organization.

While working as a customer advocate, I soon learned that a good bit of my work involved the members and their representation of the organization. Most of the time, I discovered, when "recovery" of a customer was required, it was because of issues caused by the organization's own members. As the comic strip character Pogo says, when I met the enemy, it often was "us." I saw lack of support of the organization by its own members. Members demonstrated a lack of caring about the customer and/or the work they were doing, and the customers knew it. The victimized customers perceived these members as the organization. They experienced members as not caring about them or their work, and saw these attitudes as demonstrations of the organization's attitude. They wanted to be treated better, and they let the contact people and the organization know it.

It was also clear that the majority of the members of this organization were not causing customer problems. It was a noncaring, nonperforming few that kept cropping up as poor organizational representatives, both on and off the job.

Every day, in all segments of their lives, people perform as advocates for or against the things they care about or dislike.

Those segments may include their favorite teams, close or distant relationships, social organizations, and most likely their work organizations. Performance as positive or negative advocates can directly or indirectly affect the welfare of the target of the advocacy.

Advocacy is defined as an act of pleading for, supporting, or recommending. In actuality, it has always been around. Intervening on behalf of others is a natural activity for the human endeavor. It is performed not only by an assigned person, someone responsible to promote an organization or idea, but also by everyone at one time or another.

Advocacy is an element of the consultative role of all members in the workplace community. Successful promotion of the organizational community is vital to the top performance of organizations and to the member-advocates. Being an advocate is not always easy. It may require going against the accepted norm in the organization. Finding something to advocate may require the member to reframe or look at things differently, to dig for the positives on a regular basis.

Members who willingly perform actions of advocacy are often caring, compassionate, and passionate about what they believe in. In organizations, successful advocates

- Enjoy a "working with" approach and demonstrate this enjoyment to co-members
- Care about their organization's image and success
- Are proud of the organization and the co-members they represent
- Are energized by the opportunity to serve others
- Take empowerment seriously when working with/leading with others

Such positive organizational members are not exceptional. But these days they occasionally appear to be hiding. The person who yells loudest is heard, and the counterculture is loud and clear, talking to everyone who will listen. As one CEO of a large organization said, "I overhear a lot of conversations in the cafeteria about how tough it is out there. It's become a badge of courage among workers to be tired, grumpy, and overworked." It is difficult to be courageous when you are tired, frustrated, and fearful of what is ahead. It is hard for members to believe that what they do and say matters to the bottom lines of their organizations. But, as reiterated throughout this book, members are directly or indirectly responsible for the success, stagnation, or failure of their organizations: *What we do, how we act, what we praise and what we ridicule, and what we see as consequential and inconsequential demonstrate our message of encouragement or our "wish" for the failure of our co-members, customers, and organizations.*

Obviously, performance as an advocate cannot be mandated, but negative advocacy can be an accountability (accountability is discussed in Chapter Seven). Positive advocacy performances can and should be rewarded. Conversely, coaching can help counteract negative advocacy. Members must be willing, committed participants in the advocacy process for it to be believable; they must feel a connection to their jobs, their co-members, and their organization. It is imperative for organizations to create a climate that makes advocacy possible.

But every day we hear that loyalty and commitment are gone forever. Organizations bemoan the nonexistence of the loyal, committed members of the past, who would go the extra mile every day, who stayed with their organizations through thick and thin, often ignoring the greener grass on the other side of the community fence. Such members would routinely work at getting past short-term problems.

However, many members are asking why they *should* stay with organizations that are not in turn loyal to them. They see and experience downsizing, rightsizing, reengineering, and the introduction of technology as excuses for making them work harder or for eliminating their jobs all together.

If we are the organization, why is this happening? How did elimination of jobs become necessary if we are all diligently minding the store every day of the work week? Why are members at the "bottom" of organizations so detached from the goals and purposes of their workplace communities, and why are the "tops" suddenly awakening to the need to take drastic steps to "fix" our organizations? Who was asleep at the switch here?

The answer is, everyone—every member—was asleep at the switch, hoping someone else was watching for the train coming down the track. Or perhaps everyone was distracted, basking in past successes. Everyone, from the CEO, to the management, to the professionals, to the warehouse workers, to the clerk-associates, was perpetuating mediocrity by doing just enough to appear committed. Status quo was a way of working.

Some claim that blind loyalty, plus assumptions that "they" (the president, vice presidents, directors, etc.) *knew* how to lead into the future, caused today's dilemmas. But blind loyalty has been dead for years. Members have been passing the buck *up* and forgetting to hold themselves or the leader-members to whom they passed it accountable for mediocre performance. The result has been rampant greed at the top and entitlement at the bottom. There hasn't been much to be positive about recently in many of our workplace communities.

Connection creates opportunities to consider positive advocacy gestures built on responsible, credible, and comfortable workplace relationships. Remaining isolated is difficult when you feel connected to those around you. Gestures of advocacy result from and are generated by feelings of connection, ultimately creating a cycle of advocacy that expands those connections and increases the willingness of members to continue advocacy gestures, as seen in Figure 5.

Actions of advocacy do not just happen. They are activated by an individual in order to demonstrate a personal desire to work with and lead with others in the workplace community. Gestures, when accepted as beneficial by the recipient, activate reciprocal gestures. A cycle of action, assessment, response, confirmation, reassessment, partnership, and decision to repeat generates a spiral upward in the relationship being advocated. Implicit in the model is that someone is willing to start the cycle and feel some responsibility to perpetuate the relationship.

The positive advocate is a contributing, consultative member. When members work with co-members, they make it possible to achieve mutual and individual goals. Each person consciously or unconsciously demonstrates to observers what he or she believes about the organization. Being a positive advocate often requires intentionally seeking what is good and positive about the organization and our co-members. To look for perfection is futile. To look for incidents of near perfection or comfort is realistic.

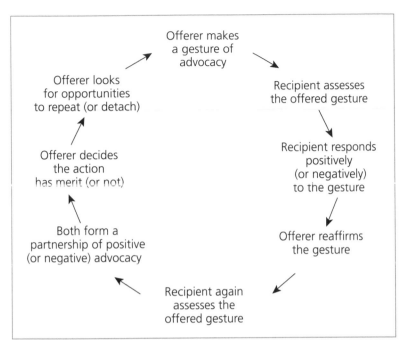

FIGURE 5   Cycle of Advocacy

The consultative role is significant to the activity of performing as an advocate. In initiating an advocacy gesture, often the responding person checks it out before accepting and moving into a partnering relationship. The advocacy cycle begins when a member approaches a co-member about a task issue. The co-member may be a peer, a leader-member, or a subordinate. The initiating member opens the issue for discussion, suggesting (offering) a partnership that could be beneficial because of the skills and knowledge of the co-member. The participants discuss the issue and the offered opportunity to partner, assess the gesture, and then respond positively or negatively to the partnership. The offerer reaffirms the gesture as a good idea, and the recipient becomes more convinced that the partnership can be beneficial. The partnership is formed, and task activity begins. The partners decide the action has been beneficial and look for opportunities to repeat the formation of partnerships—and the cycle begins again.

The gesture of advocating a person is often the same. Suspicion is rampant in our organizations, so when a member promotes someone as a good, deserving member, the receiver often will check out what is being heard. The exchange may include negative feedback that the advocate will counter with other advocacy statements, with the promoter continuing to promote the co-member as a good, deserving member. At this point, the responder will either agree, be neutral, or disagree. A positive response will validate the advocacy gestures of the promoter and affirm that the promotion is acceptable. The advocate, in assessing the activity, will decide if other opportunities of advocacy are beneficial and either repeat the role or detach from the role.

Negative gestures of advocacy stick. Even if they are proven unfounded, what is said is remembered. Negative promotion affirms suspicion and aligns persons in negative partnerships that are competitive and disconnective. Members who participate in gossip and rumor advocacy gestures are interrupting the overall group's ability to maintain pleasant and productive relationships.

Getting to comfortable happens within the context of advocacy: Each person performs or does not perform advocacy actions within community relationships. These advocacy relationships include members as marketers (organizational advocacy); the leader's role in advocating co-members (member advocacy); members advocating leader-members (leader advocacy); and customer advocacy.

Organizational Advocacy®

Organizational advocacy is defined as the willingness and responsibility of the member to positively promote his or her organization both inside and outside of the organization. A member's level of willingness and responsibility to be an advocate is a choice made individually.

In the past, members could leave their jobs at the end of the day and tell anyone who would listen how badly they were being treated, how bad the products were, and how badly the place was being managed, without, they thought, repercussions. They could sabotage their organization and still collect a paycheck. These same members were often unwilling to participate in addressing the problems they were broadcasting to the world because "it's not my job."

And the organization agreed. Management did not want to hear the concerns and challenges of the lower echelons, and if someone took the risk to say something, there was a price to pay. The "them" versus "us" mentality was accepted as normal by all participants. Members in the middle of the pyramid were the meat in the metaphorical sandwich, taking directions from the top and transposing them into actions for those at the bottom of the pyramid. Members at the bottom played their role of not knowing anything well and believed they influenced the workplace very little, negatively or positively, inside or outside of the workplace community. The farther down the pyramid, the heavier the bureaucratic load got, and no one seemed to care.

Under these circumstances, even thinking about promoting the organization, its members, or its products or services positively was farfetched, even out of the question. It was nasty out there; situations happened all day every day within organizations that made it tough. So how does the member perform as a successful organizational advocate when humans will be human?

People are more able to cope when there is acceptance and connection. Organizational advocacy is relational and includes actions and responses to relationships with others, on and off the job, as discussed in Chapter Five. Advocacy is not easy in times of uncertainty, but the cumulative gestures of advocacy are valued contributions to the potential success of workplace communities. When members are confused and wondering what they can do to support the endeavors of the organization, they can make simple, self-fulfilling gestures.

In today's working environment, all members are marketers. Current and potential customers can and do make conscious choices about where they will buy products and services based on unconscious perceptions and needs that members can influence. For the most part, the products and services provided can and are duplicated by other providers. If its product is the same, only service and ability to connect with the customer or client set an organization apart. Members directly or indirectly influence the decisions of current and potential customers.

Members are the best marketers their company has, twenty-four hours a day, on the job and off the job. To perform as a marketer for the organization is a responsibility. If the organization does not succeed, the member does not succeed. The effect of positive verbal support of the organization in conversations with friends, family, and acquaintances in everyday life is significant, and organizations need to promote awareness of the need for such organizational support. In the past, members often left their responsibility to be a contributing member at the door or gate as they left for the day. They took no responsibility for what was said after hours because "What I do and say about my company after hours is none of their business." This is seen as the right of free speech, not affecting employability.

Of course, members have the right to promote or not promote their organization. But do they have the right to go one step further and verbally sabotage the organization? Does it really matter what one person does in the scheme of organizational things? Does a person have a right to take home a paycheck from an organization but be unwilling to contribute to it in a positive way?

How members treat customers is what pays the bills. How partnerships work inside the organization is basic to the survival of the individual and the organization. Every contact with internal or external customers or clients solidifies attitudes toward the organization. Customers watch (and listen) as a service is being performed or not being performed and even participate as partners in the process. In the best of worlds, the member identifies with the customer, positively connects with the customer, and becomes committed to serving the customer, while performing in the best interest of the workplace community.

Member Advocacy

Member advocacy is a leadership responsibility. Leader-member advocates actively promote the group members to others inside and outside their group. Members, in order to perform well, must be accepted or legitimized by leader-members and co-members.

This role is a recent addition to the accountabilities of leader-members. Although it may have been an assumed or implied role, to say it is an accountability is moving the role of sponsor and advocate to a new level—a level many leaders will be uncomfortable accepting. With the exception of a brief discussion by Kuczmarski and Kuczmarski (1995) *Values-Based Leadership,* this role has not been actively addressed as a leadership norm. This is unacceptable. Leader actions and attitudes every day limit or invigorate the participation of members. It is time to hold our formal and informal leaders accountable for their disempowering actions and attitudes. Member advocacy must happen.

Leader-members' positive or negative assumptions about individual members teach others how those members should be treated and what they should expect of them. Leader actions of advocacy influence the amount of cooperation a member receives, whether he or she gets adequate information, and the amount of peer training he or she is offered. Ultimately, how successful the member will be in his or her accountabilities depends on advocacy gestures of sponsorship and support by leaders and acceptance by co-members.

Sponsorship

Acceptance of new members into the group is an emotion-based activity having to do with concern regarding reciprocal acts of acceptance and threat to the responder's well-being in the group: Will this new member displace me in the group? Will this new member change how things are done? Will I be seen by the new person as a successful, appropriate member in the group? Insecurities abound for the current member as well as for the new member. It is the role of the leader to ease the fears and concerns of both new and current group members. How or whether this is accomplished early on in the unfolding co-member relationship in the group is significant to the new member's role in the group as long as he or she is part of the group. When a member enters a new position or organization, there is a "paying your dues" time. Getting through this time can be easy or difficult. By advocating the member, the formal and informal leader can positively affect acceptance by the group.

Member advocacy tactics by the leader are relational, inclusive activities geared toward supporting, promoting, developing, creating goodwill toward, empowering, and coaching. Member advocacy responsibilities do not end after the member is hired and escorted to the job. The leader's continued efforts to *advocate* members to the group facilitate acceptance. These activities are observed by the group, influencing the group's actions and responses toward the new member. Kuczmarski and Kuczmarski (1995) say that "leaders must help employees ignite their potential, unfold and grow their intelligences, determine their most effective roles, make their jobs meaningful and self-satisfying, and endorse agreed-upon norms and values." Gestures of member advocacy matter, facilitating member success and achievement over time.

A member advocate initiates opportunities for advocacy by carefully selecting new members that he or she feels confident will be top performers. The leader is then motivated to encourage acceptance of the individual new member into the group. The leader sponsors the new member to the group and other organizational members as a capable, likeable, appropriate, and contributing person whom the group would be justified in supporting. This sponsorship activity initiates acceptance, increasing the potential of performance by the new member and the group.

The leader-member does not advocate the member once and then step out; rather, he or she reinforces the worthiness of the new member over time, making it possible for the member as well as the group to continue to merge and become productive and cohesive. These actions of sponsorship are different from performing as a mentor (discussed in the next section) in that they are ongoing, tied to membership in the leader's group, and open to observation by the group. The differences between sponsorship and mentorship are seen in Chart 16.

A sponsor is one who vouches for or is responsible for a person or thing and makes promises for, vouches for, or answers for that person or thing. A mentor, on the other hand, is a wise and

CHART 16   Sponsorship vs. Mentorship

Sponsorship	Mentorship
Automatic responsibility	Voluntary responsibility
Professional relationship	May be a personal relationship
Highly visible	Not always visible
Internal to the organization	May be external to the organization
Advocacy/coaching role	Counseling/guiding role
Long-term relationship	Now based
Acceptance and development issue	Growth issue

trusted counselor. Sponsorship is a more direct, connected activity. The sponsor is responsible for the person he or she is sponsoring, and the leader does not choose to sponsor; intervention and direct, visible support by the leader-member on behalf of the member is now an assigned function of leadership. However, although many organizations are actively using mentoring as a tool for development of their new and promising members, most organizations are not introducing the long-term approach that includes expanded sponsorship as an accountability of the leader.

Sponsorship assumes that the overall membership group, even an individual co-member, can have an effect on the success of the organization. French and Bell (1990) say that "most individuals have drives toward personal growth and development if provided an environment that is both supportive and challenging" (p. 44). When these drives are strong in an individual or group and sponsorship is encouraged, expected, and supported by the organization, a positive psychological contract between parties for higher achievement and cooperation will develop. Expectations of performance become more person focused for both.

A leader can also delegitimize a member. A skeptical comment to someone else; a thoughtless response to the member, observed by co-members; an inappropriate explosion in front of others; a cynical response when the member is trying to make a point; or sharing with others "concerns" about the member that may or may not be valid—are all delegitimizing and devaluing tactics that happen almost unconsciously. If a member, group, and organization are to be as successful as possible, these tactics are to be avoided.

Advocating Members to Leader-Members

Advocacy responsibilities of the leader include the promotion of the best interests of members to the leader's peer group. The leader-member positively represents members to other leaders as top performers (when appropriate) who deserve the trust of the leader group. The leader also must promote or stand up for members when problems arise. The leader-member assures the group of the competence of the member, easing problems and consequences when a member is struggling (or having a learning event).

Attesting to the competence of a member may also open opportunities for future growth and performance for the member. Advocating exemplary performers (as opposed to holding them back to retain their talents) keeps capable members in the organization and promotes feelings of significance regarding their role in the organization. Many members are their leader's best-kept secret; no one outside the group knows about their exemplary performance. After all, think about the consequences to the leader's own accountabilities if the top-performing member were to move on.

Consider the following positive example: Recently I was on a plane and overheard a conversation between two seatmates who worked for Moen Incorporated—Jim Yezbak, vice president of retail sales, and Shannon Akin Thomas, supervisor of in-store service. It became obvious that what I was overhearing was a true example of leader-sponsorship and co-member validation. They were describing the fine qualities of a person reporting to Yezbak and the confidence both had that he would do a good job on a planned presentation.

The described subordinate was in direct contact with external customers and was well accepted and respected by both his internal and external customers. Yezbak said, "X is looking for someone in [city]. Although I hate to lose him, the company needs good people like him. I am hoping they will consider him for the position." (Yes, I introduced myself, admitted I was listening, and asked their permission to tell this story.)

Yezbak's demonstrated activities of sponsorship and Thomas's willingness to validate the abilities of member X activate the potential of a top performer who could have been held hostage by a leader who was unwilling to lose a good, productive performer. The potential of high-performing members who are actively sponsored is unshackled by leaders who see the benefit in providing opportunities for their growth instead of creating frustration for them.

Leader-member advocates also "work with" when it is necessary to short-circuit inefficient processes. In the Membership Organization, with lines blurred and status no longer a barrier, members have permission to create partnerships across the circle to bring all available expertise to the table. These partnerships expand the feelings of competence, empowerment, and significance and open opportunities to ask questions (challenge) and to share knowledge liberally. Thus growth opportunities are created for all participants, those offering advocacy and those receiving the advocacy gestures.

Leader Advocacy

Leader advocacy is a responsibility of all members across the organizational circle. Actions of co-members in supporting and promoting the leader as competent, desirable, and beneficial to the organizational group are important to the leader's ability to perform. Members who advocate initiate a flow of understanding directed toward the leader. These leader advocacy statements travel through the organizational circle in the form of stories and rumors. What is said and done represents the leader to others, verifying the leader-member as appropriate in the role. Conversely, to negatively promote the leader is easy and may generate quick approval from members who have in the past been disconnected and unappreciative of the expertise needed to lead groups, departments, and organizations.

No matter where leaders work in the organization, they may feel isolated and disconnected. Because leaders are human, these feelings of disconnection may nurture their own doubts about their competence. When members do not support the leader, leader-members may burn out. Harry Levinson (1996) quoted a leader as saying, "In my role, I'm the guy who catches it all. I don't know how much longer I can last in this job" (p. 153). Isolation is devastating. The co-members who leave their leaders to carry the burden alone, without offering assistance and support on a regular basis, are setting them up to struggle. Speaking in trusted confidence about issues and concerns—or just talking about the Pittsburgh Steelers—lessens the likelihood of the leader's burnout. Members must stop looking for the perfect, most relational leader, the rescuer, and support the ones already in place. Making it possible for the leader to succeed makes it possible for everyone to succeed.

Here is an example of how leader advocacy can work: A member was at a dinner party and a friend asked, "What is it like working for [her boss]? I hear he is pretty tough to work for. What do you say?" The member's response set him back: "I really enjoy working with him because I respect him a lot. He is brilliant, a spokesman in our industry, and has taken a small company to a medium-sized one in a very short time. He has also taught me a lot—and allowed me to do and learn things that I never would have had an opportunity to do with another boss. It has been an amazing experience, and it means a lot to me to be working with him."

The questioner was so impressed with the response that several months later he told the boss about the conversation. The following day, the boss mentioned to the member his appreciation for her comments. The member had positively advocated the organizational leader and the message had gotten back and was appreciated, even by the "tough boss."

Customer Advocacy

Member actions of customer advocacy, like organizational advocacy, are a must for organizations hoping to survive in the twenty-first century. All members in customer contact roles are customer advocates, representing their organization while working with customers in order to meet their needs. (Although focusing on external customers, actions of customer advocacy are also linked to performance in serving internal customers of the organizational member.) The following characteristics of the customer advocate role are in addition to the general characteristics of the advocate discussed earlier in this chapter. The customer advocate

- Cares about the welfare of the organization's customers
- Knows that satisfied customers mean job security
- Is willing to positively represent the organization to the customer
- Actively represents the customer's needs to the organization
- Is trained and willing to make appropriate decisions on the spot to meet the needs of organizational customers

This list implies that customer advocacy is an influencing responsibility. No matter how great an organization's potential, no matter how good its product or service, it is the influencing abilities of members at all levels that determine its success. Three automatic member influencing activities suggest that top performance as a customer advocate is a specific responsibility of each individual member:

1. *Members cannot* not *communicate their feelings and perceptions about the customer or the organization.* Ideal customer contact people truly enjoy opportunities to work with external organizational customers. They are willing stewards and advocates of their organization and their customers, in every phase of their life. These same outlooks create an atmosphere of trust in their work associations and in their willingness to contribute to the effectiveness of the organizational community.

2. *Members cannot* not *influence customers about their organization.* Members are seen, until proven otherwise, as credible representatives of the organization and as such influence the perceptions of the current or potential customer. Willingly accepting personal responsibility for how service is delivered to each customer contributes to each member's ability to influence customers both inside and outside the organization.

3. *Members cannot* not *evaluate their own organization through the eyes of the customer.* The cycle of understanding starts with members and can in return create or expand feelings of member pride or concern (or shame) about their organization. Insinuations and messages, delivered consciously or unconsciously by members to customers, create good or bad customer images and expectations of the organization. The tone of voice, indications of trust or distrust, and amount of enthusiasm and cooperation members use with customers teach customers what to think about the organization and its product or service. Positive or negative responses by customers initiate corresponding responses for the member. The member has initiated a cycle of influence. This evaluation process is automatic.

These influencing mechanisms are affected by "facts" that have been accepted by customers in the last decade, facts that have become entitlements for service that must be met in order to gain and retain customers. New measurements of performance for organizational contact persons emphasize the need for members to be customer advocates.

Fact #1:
At a minimum, customers expect members to be positive about their own organization and the people they work with while they deliver excellent service and exceptional products.

Each member is a representative of the organization. Customers expect members to confirm, through their actions and words, that they have chosen the right organization. Who would know better than the person who works for that organization?

Fact #2:
Every day, with every contact, customers decide the future of both the member and the organization.

The customer sees and understands the organization through the eyes of the member. It has been said that when we think no one is looking, everyone is looking. With every gesture, both on and off the job, members are creating impressions of competence or incompetence about their work, their organization, and the product or service provided by their organization.

Fact #3:
Organizational representatives are experts no matter where they work in the organizational circle. The expertise of the advocate in representing the customer to the organization must be heeded in order to best serve the customer.

This fact reflects a welcome recognition of the hands-on knowledge and expertise at the edges of organizations. When members are seen as knowing their jobs, it affects their feelings of significance and competence, which in turn affect basic loyalty issues of belonging, acceptance, and recognition. The excellence and quality processes being initiated in organizations are, if they are succeeding, using experts throughout the circle to identify the improvements needed to become both local and global competitors in the marketplace. The day of the organizational member has arrived, wherever he or she is in the circle.

Fact #4:
Positive customer-influencing activities performed internally and externally are a responsibility of each member in the organization.

No matter how great an organization's potential, it is the influencing abilities and opportunities of the organization's members when working with customers that makes organizational growth and success possible. Such member influence requires the demonstration of positive attitudes and actions of advocacy toward both the customer and the member's organization.

Organizational Responsibility

The organization's role in advocacy is to provide members an environment that makes it possible and appropriate for them to be advocates for their workplace community. If they are stifled, ignored, left to fend for themselves, treated unfairly, and encouraged to assume that managers always know what to do, or worse, that they do not want to be told by the "less-thans" that something is amiss, then members will be comatose on the job. They will not contribute to their full ability, nor will they perform actions of advocacy for the organization, its members, or its products or services, on or off the job. Of course, knowing *what* to do is different from knowing how to do it. It is a challenge to the organizational system to become a Membership Organization. And because "we are the organization," all members influence how to make it happen.

But advocacy gestures, both internal and external, are not mandatable—the member must make an individual decision to perform as a positive advocate. Because the organization has to design, reinforce, and support an environment that nurtures actions of advocacy by all members, change is not achieved overnight, and a necessary ingredient is the willingness of the collective membership to participate in the process. It is not appropriate that members not assume responsibility for or be unwilling to perpetuate the high-energy, top-performing, advocacy-oriented organization. *All members are responsible for the climate of the organization, and all members participate in the process of initiation and perpetuation of the organization, which cannot succeed to its potential without advocacy gestures.* In order to create the right climate, each member has to perceive the need and see advocacy as beneficial.

To illustrate the point, here is an example: Bob Huff, a Cincinnati, Ohio, labor-management consultant with a union background, believes that organizations are "perfectly designed for the results they get." The new union environment of today sees that the union and its members can be successful only if the company is successful. The majority of the workers at all levels of the workplace community want to be proud of their organization—proud enough that they would be willing to positively promote their organization both on and off the job. Whether union or not, when members find opportunities to tap into skills that have lain dormant and use new learnings to contribute, they also find pride—pride in their work, in their organization, and in themselves and their co-members. When pride is reawakened, ownership happens. All members across the organizational circle must work together to make this possible.

Individual Responsibility

Each person decides whether he or she is going to be a positive or negative advocate for the organization. The decision promotes behaviors in the workplace that are learned and enacted over the long term. Consultant Sherene Zolno (1996) states, "My experience is that how members talk about their work is an indication of whether they believe in it. Also, their conversations about their work determine whether they deserve to get the resources that they crave." What members say influences whether they get opportunities to succeed. When a member chooses negative advocacy, it takes time and patience to replace those behaviors with multiple beneficial behaviors (if it can be done at all), and it takes willing, direct, personal involvement of co-members to create changes.

For members struggling with advocacy, their responsibility to promote their organization is hard to swallow. They may say, I wasn't hired in marketing or sales; I'm not being paid after five o'clock to promote the company; they don't care what I say anyway; ten years ago (something) happened and I don't want to say anything good about this company; I die ten thousand times a day in this place. Such comments are all too common in organizations, making it difficult for co-workers to maintain patience while these members decide to become, or not become, positive advocates for their organization. Such members often see success as performing gestures of negative advocacy. But whereas it can't hurt to contribute positively to the company even in the smallest ways, it surely can hurt if you don't. In some cases, all you can hope for is their silence.

Positive advocacy has direct impact on members' attitudes and on the attitudes of people around them. An individual willingly participating in an advocacy role can make a difference in the environment. In fact, participation as an advocate has many advantages for the member, including

- Increasing the member's pride in the organization
- Increasing member credibility both on and off the job
- Increasing trust and acceptance by customers
- Opening channels of information and communication with co-members, making it possible to better achieve, whatever the level of performance
- Increasing personal and professional growth that can provide opportunities for increased empowerment and participation

In a positive atmosphere of advocacy, each member benefits as well as the organization. Member attitudes make or break the atmosphere of advocacy and are influenced by the member's viewpoints and his or her acceptance or nonacceptance of the responsibility of performing as an advocate on the job.

> Fact #5:
> Membership stops where a member's actions or comments about the organization affect others in a way that puts the organization (and the membership) at risk.

Aside from issues of ethics, a member's verbally jeopardizing or sabotaging his or her own organization is essentially saying, "My organization should not exist." Members' negative actions of advocacy in effect tell customers or clients they should take their business elsewhere. When members have concerns, they have three options. They can (1) be proactive in bringing positive change to the organization (challenge in the right way); (2) leave and find an organization they can believe in (or wait for the organization to leave them); or (3) abide by the old saying, "If you don't have anything nice to say, don't say anything." Unfortunately, when members don't say anything, they are probably unconsciously saying it all.

Summary

Actions of advocacy, whether they be performances of organizational advocacy, member advocacy, leader advocacy, or customer advocacy, are now more important than ever. The success of large and small organizations alike may hang in the balance, based on the comments of a single member. Internal and external customers are watching for messages of concern or unconcern and support or nonsupport regarding the organization's interest, as projected by members. These messages directly and indirectly affect the organization's efforts to survive and thrive.

Members' performance as advocates both within and outside organizations affects all three bottom lines. This is explicitly why advocacy may in the future become an accountability, not a choice. Whether it is the social bottom line, the human bottom line, or the financial bottom line, sustaining organizations requires members to be responsible, ethical, and proactive in addressing issues in organizations. If all members actively accept the responsibility to improve their organization, advocacy happens. Members gain pride in what they have created, they assume ownership of the goals and achievements of the organization, and the results are actions of advocacy for the organization that the members together are in the process of constructing.

9

Each of us . . . [has] to become a
creator of the organization to which
we belong. It may even be our job
to teach those above us how an
effective community is created. We,
in fact, become the customers of
our bosses. We create in our unit
what we would like to see embod-
ied in the whole organization!

Peter Block,
Empowering People in Organizations

The Membership

Coach Jimmy Valvano said in a speech shortly before his death, "I see a good life as lived by doing three things every day: laugh, think, and cry. It's an eventful day—you can't be bored."

This concept of a good life is eventful—and it is a way of living that people appreciate as appropriate *outside of the workplace*. Every day in real-world living, people laugh, think, and cry with families, friends, store clerks, fast food servers, and so on. Unfortunately, these behaviors do not always transfer to the workplace community.

At work, members allow themselves to laugh a little and think (and do) as necessary, but no one is allowed to cry (disagree). To disagree, stand up for what you believe, and be emotional in the process is "inappropriate." Everyone expects his or her workplace community to be perfect, so all members must disagree quietly, if at all, and not speak the unspeakable; they must nod agreement to those with status and do their own job, unquestioningly. It is appropriate to be consultative (participative) only when asked—and then only within the boundaries of the "acceptable." Tolerance is limited and to be human is to err—unforgivably. The questioning, even emotional member, is an under-functioning member. Perfection is expected and imperfection is intolerable.

In the past, the functioning member supplied effort, loyalty, and productivity to the organization and in return expected loyalty. There was an unspoken, psychological "if-then" contract: *If* I work hard and do at least the minimum, *then* the organization will honor its end of the bargain and keep me on the job. This led to the scenario that *if* the contract was violated by the person, *then* the organization had the right to take action; *if* the contract was violated by the organization, *then* the member felt betrayed (quietly) and left or withheld full input in his or her work.

These unspoken contracts became the foundations for the individual's identity inside and outside the workplace. Members created life goals and futures based on assumptions that the contract would not change, no matter how the environment changed for the organization. They adopted this job and this organization as their own. Complacency set in. Many people worked on automatic pilot. Life drained out of their jobs and they no longer looked for opportunities to be challenged or to initiate ways their organization could do things differently or better. Status quo and apathy became a way of work life.

The questions to be asked are, when members become apathetic and their workplace becomes a status quo community, is it a healthy, thriving organization? Is it possible under these conditions for the member to take ownership of and be enrolled in the organizational purpose? If the answer is no or maybe or I really don't know, it is time to be concerned—wherever the answering member stands in the organizational circle. These questions can reveal the potential for productivity and health in the workplace community.

Membership: An Overarching Design

The concept of membership in organizations is not new. However, the concept of a framework or structure that is built around shared principles and significant language *is* new.

The questions loom: Can the framework of membership provide guiding principles for working together in the real world of organizations? Is it possible to work together for the common good of all members *and* the organization? Or is the membership organization a utopian dream that cannot be achieved in the workplace community of the twenty-first century?

In today's chaotic environment, the challenge is to encourage the workplace community to look at what can realistically be achieved through membership, then consider those possibilities in relation to what is happening in the workplace community now. Another question to consider: Could it be that all gestures of withdrawal, avoidance, and disruption are a yearning for acceptance and involvement, for appreciation as a contributing, valued member of an organization that members *want* to see succeed (Srivastva & Barrett, 1990)? If so, perhaps there is no choice but to consider alternatives to the organizing scenarios in place today.

William Bridges (1991) states, "It is important for you to have— or to create—an overarching design to the symphony of change. Without such an overall design, every little change will sound like an unrelated melody that must be started or stopped without regard to the rest of the music" (p. 71). As such, the Membership Organization (1) offers an "overarching design," (2) uses a language that is a mobilizing metaphor for change within organizations, (3) provides symbolism that makes it possible to create new realities and new logic, and (4) is a structure making connection possible within the workplace community.

Membership is a mind-set, requiring open, ongoing, communitywide dialogue about what creates top performance. All members need to talk about being trusted and trustworthy and being responsible and accountable. Through dialogue, members learn their role in creating an environment of inclusive independence and interdependence. All members learn the expectations of performance in the new workplace community and share their own expectations and concerns.

Community

In the new workplace community of the Membership Organization, pride and commitment expand through shared, understood responsibility and accountability, challenging the organization as a community to continually grow through addressing the needs of the membership, the customer, and the organization as a whole. Questions are asked; reasons are sought; and active listening across the circle helps identify crucial issues. The outcome is the expansion of all three bottom lines and the vision that those bottom lines will continue to expand.

Traditional bureaucratic organizations use position descriptions to establish limits to involvement and responsibility, instructing members to "keep your ideas to yourself—that's his area." When co-members are forced to keep their thoughts to themselves, the next step is blaming. Something went wrong when an idea wasn't heard or an alternative wasn't investigated—because no one was interested. This leads to frustration and isolation, reaffirming the barriers within the bureaucratic organization. It could have been done better, the member thinks, knowing the pattern will be repeated again and again. In order to interrupt this "quiet desperation," something has to give.

The healing can begin with blurring the lines between organizational relationships while actively building connections that work, thus establishing new, exciting partnerships across the circle (see Chapter Five). These new relationships must be based on acceptance and acknowledgment as well as belief in and commitment to the concepts of community (see Chapter One). A nurturing community generates feelings of respect, concern, connection, responsibility, self-worth, capability, empowerment, and ownership. Gifford Pinchot (1996) states, "Community is a phenomenon that occurs most easily when free people with some sense of equal worth join together voluntarily for a common enterprise" (p. 28).

The voluntariness of the Membership Organization and the expansion of the inner circle to the edges initiates opportunities for a vision of communal self-worth, enrolling members in the purpose of their workplace community. Members of the workplace community actively pursue the expansion and growth of their community together through empowerment, alignment, assumption of leadership, and advocacy.

Empowerment. Empowerment requires personal, partnership, and organizational decisioning that is made possible through inclusive independence and interdependence. Empowerment also provides the impetus for all members to make the choice to actively invest in the future for themselves, their group, and their community.

Alignment. The members align themselves to the best interests of their community and the customers they serve, both inside and outside the organization. As a result, productive, flexible partnerships create opportunities for success for the organization and for the members within the aligned partnerships.

Assumption of leadership. Community building encourages leaders to emerge from the crowd. The priority of hiring the right people and making it possible for them to be top performers through sponsorship, development, and training enables members to build feelings of significance. These feelings generate energy and vitality that contribute to the bottom lines of the Membership Organization.

Advocacy. Members who experience significance through competency, empowerment, and challenge are willing advocates both within and outside their organizations (as discussed in Chapter Eight). In the old way of working, pride was manifested by withholding criticism and "not seeing" the organization's need for improvement. Pride and enrollment expand in the new workplace community when members sense that their organization values their input and involvement.

The "Givens" of Membership

There are some "givens" that are understood, believed in, and committed to by community members when change agents are slow-jump-starting a membership environment. Slow-jump-starting involves introducing new assumptions in ways that encourage discussion and questions, without suggesting that the assumptions are modifiable. Of course, "slow" is relative to some leader-members anxious for change to occur. For others it would be too fast. The point is not to attack but to move into a new approach, to make a smooth transition while actively, purposefully making simultaneous changes that matter across the organization.

CHART 17   The "Givens" of Membership

- The Principles of Membership are the guiding forces behind the establishment of a new way to work.

- Members are creating a more level working community together; it cannot happen otherwise.

- Empowerment is fundamental to deep participation in the organizational community.

- Members are forgiven when failure happens.

- High levels of individual and group responsibility and accountability are important to the success of the Membership Organization.

A smooth transition is less threatening, inviting members to become partners in the new assumptions of how to achieve both as individuals and as a community. Inviting starts with the recognition that there is historical and current "good" in organizations that must be perpetuated.

But organizations need clear messages that serve as impetus and direction, underlining new ground rules for how work is to be done from now on (Tetlock, 1990). Such messages define and publicize where the workplace community is going. A sample of the givens or premises for the introduction of the Membership Organization are seen in Chart 17. (Each organization would enroll its own members to identify its own.

The Principles of Membership are the guiding forces behind the establishment of a new way to work. The interdependencies of the Membership Organization are established through empowerment of individuals and partnerships, giving members a stronger sense of stability during the change process. The Principles of Membership create a new sense of hope—which in turn provides the foundation for a new community.

Members are creating this more level working community together; it cannot happen otherwise. Wherever individuals are located in the workplace community, they are interdependent, synergistic, and dynamic in creating an organizational future. In a Membership Organization, everyone contributes to the bottom lines of the organization. Although elimination of status is not possible, the mind-set of having "less-thans" and "more-thans" within the organization can and must be changed. Blurring the status lines is essential to the achievement of a membership environment. Through education and training, the membership perspective can encourage individual learning about the organizational challenges and goals, the member's role in them, and what top individual and group performance can mean to the bottom lines.

Empowerment is fundamental to deep participation in the organizational community. Lowered boundaries and barriers to cooperation and connection make it possible to define a future never before considered possible, a future in which all members have a voice in the organization's achievement. Lowered boundaries encourage members to lead when it is appropriate to do so. In their own areas of expertise, they are capable, resourceful, knowledgeable, accountable, and responsible, making it possible to educate and challenge them to grow while encouraging them to think as well as do. The most innovative expert may be at the next desk or machine. His or her consultative abilities are vital resources for the organization. Members are the workplace community's best resource for organizational growth; it is not necessary to be from fifty miles away to be an expert. It is important for leader-members to understand that deep participation is more successful than delegating or just asking for suggestions.

Members are forgiven when failure happens. It is understood that there is no perfect member, solution, or method and that members will not always meet the expectations of their co-members. When all members are empowered to take risks, they will occasionally misjudge an outcome. When leader-members encourage innovation while demonstrating that individuals and partnerships can expand innovation, they show that it is okay to stretch. Membership makes failure a permissible learning event to be forgiven at every level in the organizational circle. Such events trigger and strengthen sponsorship and coaching partnerships that make learning possible for both participants.

High levels of individual and group responsibility and accountability are important to the success of the Membership Organization. Respect, productivity, and enrollment increase a member's sense of responsibility and accountability in the workplace. A member's desire for higher levels of responsibility addresses the human need factors of connection, acceptance, and performance, increasing the desire to work well with others and to address membership issues in the right way. Opportunities for new levels of credibility and achievement are the outcomes of the new gestures of responsibility and accountability, as seen in Chapter Seven. Avoiding issues of responsibility and accountability in the workplace community eventually isolates and separates members, fostering disconnection.

Members signal acceptance or nonacceptance of the envisioned future organization by their willingness to take ownership of the transition process. Acceptance signals are an outcome of successful, connecting relationships across the organizational circle that ebb and flow across blurred lines. Significant to these relationships are effective, connecting membership styles—members still seek effective leader-members, and leaders still seek co-members, desiring to enroll in the purpose of the workplace community. Kouzes and Posner (1993) state, "People do vote—with their energy, their dedication, their loyalty, their talent, their actions" (p. 8). Tentative applications of new learnings and new enrollment behaviors are demonstrations of each person's willingness to invest and to risk new involvements and deeper levels of participation, ultimately trying out new ways of working.

Activating Membership

Activation of membership as a way to work creates meaningful work and healthy work relationships. But the Membership Organization does not just appear. It is the responsibility of leader-members and change agents throughout the community to initiate and cultivate an atmosphere in which membership is possible. In partnership, these leaders initiate, promote, sponsor, encourage, and support the process and the members who early on practice the membership concept. They also understand that it will take patience and dedication over time to make it happen, one person at a time.

Achieving a community that nurtures membership requires realistic expectations regarding acceptance of the philosophy of deep participation and blurred lines within the organizational circle. Known and unknown change agents, leader chosen and members self-identified, must be active in the transition process without turning people off or stimulating gestures of compliance (I'll just do what makes me look like I've enrolled). These change agents must be chosen and enrolled at all levels, spreading the concepts to the edges of the circle. Change agents must understand that the transition will involve patience and understanding coupled with determination and perseverance. To suddenly say "We are now a Membership Organization" is to doom membership to being just another flavor of the month.

Just Be It

Membership behaviors flow from a value system that will be member designed over time based on the Principles of Membership. In order for the new system to become part of the culture, leader-members must model positive, appropriate values, beliefs, and strategies that support membership.

Mutual identification of values is not an essential element of bringing about change. In the majority of the organizations that have elaborate meetings, discussing values and talking the talk, afterward everyone says, That's done. They asked questions and we told them what they wanted to hear; now we can get back to work. And they work the same way as before. Signs displaying the new values (which no one looks at) go up on the wall and the new, meaningless value statements are printed on business cards and uniforms and truck doors and become fodder for jokes and cynicism by members and customers. The reality is that signs and printed slogans, produced prematurely, breed an expectation of perfection and inevitably emphasize normal failures, and those failures solidify cynicism. There will be time for the signs—after buy-in of the membership, leading to eventual belief by the customers. Chart 18 shows realistic ways of introducing new values.

Tell the members what the ideal values are to become a Membership Organization. Give members a set of believable values that reflect the behaviors needed to be successful in the organization of the future. And tell everyone face to face. Have the

---

CHART 18   Introducing New Membership Values

- Tell the members what the ideal values are to become a Membership Organization.

- In talking about organizational values, include the concept of *being it.*

- Encourage and expect performance that reflects these beliefs from change partners and top-performing members.

- Encourage each member to participate in planning what the organization will look like in the future.

- Revisit the values as a group regularly.

- Validate, reward, and suport membership actions at all levels.

---

message delivered by people with whom they work every day and whom they see demonstrate those values on a daily basis— their leader-members (assuming the existence of trusted leader-members).

It is not beneficial to preach to a crowd of hundreds or through a video in huge meetings. Convince their direct leader, get his or her buy-in, and then send that leader-member to connect directly to the concerns and challenges of his or her co-members regarding the Principles of Membership. Training of the members must also happen—introduce them to the new values their leader is expecting to become part of the way they work and give them a reason to do so. Tie these values to the "givens" (assumptions) that have been designed by co-members, providing a foundation, design, or framework members can revert back to when uncomfortable. Although active core leader-member involvement is essential, members inevitably will be more convinced by the actions of their formal and informal leader-members, with whom they work every day.

After the message has been delivered, there is no turning back. If their direct leader implies, even in jest, that this is another management joke, members will take his or her word for it.

*In talking about organizational values, include the concept of **being it,*** committing to those values over time. The leader-members must *be* what they are promoting as right for the membership. (As co-members, there are no separate guidelines for their behavior and performance.) If leader-members are not hiring, promoting, and rewarding according to their announced new standards, co-members will notice. Gestures of living or not living the Principles, including the willingness to address blatant nonperformance of the advocated new way of working, will be under scrutiny. When leaders acknowledge their own failures, members will consider such acknowledgments. (Nobody is perfect, remember?) An apology can work miracles, humanizing members who in the past may have appeared to have a superiority complex.

Encourage and expect performance that reflects these beliefs from change partners and top-performing members. It is important that top performers and informal leaders follow through on the values as a demonstration of the way to work successfully in the organization. For the most part, top-performing members do so because they are open to change and willing to take risks. Informal leaders may or may not be top performers, so it may require special effort to enroll them in the concepts of membership. Encouraging them to be change agents and open participants in the membership transition will encourage others to accept the new way of working.

Encourage each member to participate in planning what the organization will look like in the future. Of significance is the process to be used in getting members' input for this picture. The messages received by the membership are vital to the process of change. "Inquiring into the future" must include messages of (1) the future being created together (hope), (2) acceptance and appreciation of the individual, (3) honoring of the nonrational and intuitive, and (4) awareness of people as infinite facilitators of concerns *and* possibilities (Hammond, 1996; Oliphant, 1996).

Revisit the values as a group regularly. This doesn't mean beating members over the head with them. Nor does it mean this revisiting must be done early in the introduction process, unless it is done as a part of the inquiry process in the previous step. The inclusion of members across the circle in the examination of the values and their appropriateness is important. This is an opportunity for a reality check regarding community values, and it deepens acceptance while expanding voice.

Finally, validate, reward, and support membership actions at all levels. To initiate membership tactics and not reward for moving beyond participation, participating effectively in teams, performing as advocates, or accepting new decisioning opportunities is to invalidate what the Membership Organization is about. Supporting and validating membership actions means conscious being aware of and initiatiing ways to involve the members in running the organization. As an example, member involvement in a new recognition and reward system is imperative to the acceptance of the new way of working—and is a demonstration of the concepts of membership in action. Members will be watching. Take action and remain in action as leaders and participants in the process—or the system will be seen as just another management "here today, gone tomorrow" change process. Successful forums of involvement must happen quickly.

It is the leaders' role to keep hope alive when change is happening. Supportive relationships and actions of validation keep the process credible. When the members are struggling with the change, the core leaders' involvement in and substantiation of what is occurring decrease ambiguity and uncertainty. Fear is lessened, and the illusion of stability is increased. The leader group's activities supporting the tenets of the new workplace community and the Principles of Membership (see Chapter One) are significant to the collective membership's responses to the change.

There is an interrelatedness of the components of the membership process that, when encouraged by leaders, expands membership involvement in bringing success. The relevance of these interdependencies is reliant on the level of acceptance of the proposed change by members across the circle. Reichers, Wanous, and Austin (1997) tell us that "25–40 percent of the work force will probably respond cynically to the next announcement of planned change. . . ." This realization provides leader-members an opportunity to focus on communication, training, and involvement, while knowing that there will be those who put up barriers, and that they should expect imperfection in the responses of members to the change. Moving ahead in spite of those responses is easier when one accepts the probabilities of resistance. Examples of the linking of components affected by positive interrelatedness include the following:

- *Development linkages*—The potential of the organization is brought to fruition through the development of organizational members. A significant investment in training is essential to top performance (and employability) of the members, raising the awareness of and skills in the business, technical, and intellectual areas of individual and partnership contribution to organizational success.
- *Partnership linkages, both internally and externally*—The significance of interdependent relationships is expanded by the realization that partnerships across the levels of the circle are high-performance opportunities. Task achievement, communication, rapport, informality, and connection are all enhanced by the existence of visible and invisible, temporary and permanent partnerships across the circle.
- *Cooperation of the linkages*—Cooperative linkages of processes and relationships, not domination or conformity of any group, status, or activity, increase actions of participation and interdependence while allowing for independent achievement.
- *Sustaining innovating linkages*—consistency of commitment to creativity and innovation is dependent on development, partnerships, cooperation, and the willingness to risk over time. Innovation is expanded through mutual knowledge that what each member does is significant to the success of themselves, others, and their organization.
- *Bottom-line linkages*—Linking the three bottom lines for long-term decisioning is a classic example of linking in the membership process. The Membership Organization, in considering the effect of decisions on the human, social, and financial bottom lines, increases the appropriateness of decisioning and the effect decisions have on the full community over time.

The interconnecting linkages of the components of the membership process are innumerable. Everything that is done or said has a ripple effect that touches other actions and responses. The ripple moves inward as well as outward, from the core and to the core of the circle, re-emphasizing the idea that every member has a role, a responsibility, and an accountability in affecting the success or failure of the organizational community. The input of each member, whether positive or negative, is recognized as relevant to the response his or her action causes. Being cynical makes leader-generated hope difficult to accept or sustain. Being a positive member adds value to our own abilities to contribute to the organization, to self-motivate, to lead others, to have meaningful relationships, to make decisions of value, to be responsible and accountable for what we do, and to affect the success of our company and others through promotion.

Summary

It is obvious that merely rethinking the way organizations are structured will not in itself transform existing organizations; however, rethinking how *people* think and the language they use to redesign their own thought processes may *begin* the transformation (Hall, 1996). It is also obvious that the last thing leader-members need is a new theory. The purpose of this book is to offer practical ideas, not unachievable and unrealistic theories. The consultant's challenge is to remain the coach and not the expert, a learner rather than a teacher. But there is a new sense of urgency in our organizations. Members at all levels have pressures of time, work overload that becomes information overload, and ever-increasing needs for decisioning-based inclusive independence and interdependence. There is a sense of urgency about "how things work around here," and it won't go away. It is time, as Charles Handy (1989) suggests, for new "imaginings" and for identifying new ways of facing our changed workplace reality. For some, the Membership Organization can make individual and organizational top-performance part of that reality.

The Membership Organization is possible if co-members across the circle understand that the workplace community is full of humans and as a result can never be perfect. Organizations can be cohesive, compassionate, cooperative, and collaborative *if humans are allowed to be human*. When this happens, the workplace community will, as coach Jimmy Valvano notes, be a place where people laugh, think (and do), and cry (disagree). It will be an informal place in which inclusiveness and empowerment expand to the edges, connections and partnerships prevail, gestures of advocacy become automatic, and all three bottom lines of organizations are enhanced. "We are the organization" can be an understanding arising from deep participation of all members. Of course, each day will not be perfect, but it also will not be boring.

It is somewhat simplistic to say that for all members to be competent, empowered, challenged, and significant is a huge leap in the right direction—but it is the final message of this book. An organization that accepts this challenge, while successfully expanding the inner circle to the edges, will automatically be striding toward becoming a Membership Organization. Members will *want* to be there, even if they *have* to be there.

References

Albrecht, K. (1979). *Stress and the manager: Making it work for you.* New York: Simon & Schuster.

Allcorn, S. (1994). *Anger in the workplace: Understanding the causes of aggression and violence.* Westport, CT: Quorum Books.

Argyris, C. (1990). *Overcoming organizational defenses: Facilitating organizational learning.* Needham Heights, MA: Allyn & Bacon.

Bardwick, J. M. (1991). *Danger in the comfort zone: From boardroom to the mailroom—How to break the entitlement habit that's killing American business.* New York. AMACOM.

Bellman, G. M. (1990). *The consultant's calling: Bringing who you are to what you do.* San Francisco: Jossey-Bass.

Bellman, G. M. (1992). *Getting things done when you are not in charge.* San Francisco: Berrett-Koehler.

Block, Peter (1995). Foreword. In P. McLagan & C. Nel, *The age of participation: New governance for the workplace and the world.* San Francisco: Berrett-Koehler.

Block, P. (1995, Winter). Empowering people in organizations. *Learning 2001, 6* (1), 3–5.

Bracey, H., & Smith, W. (1992, Dec. 6). The new contract. *Executive Excellence, 6.*

Bridges, W. (1991). *Managing transitions: Making the most of change.* Reading, MA: Addison-Wesley.

Brion, J. M. (1996). *Leadership of organizations: The executive's complete handbook: Part III.* Greenwich, CT: JAI Press.

Brousseau, K. R., Driver, M. J., Eneroth, K., & Larsson, R. (1996). Career pandemonium: Realigning organizations and individuals. *Academy of Management Executive, X*(4), 52–66.

Carr, C. (1993). *Smart training.* New York: McGraw-Hill.

Chaleff, I. (1996). *The courageous follower: Standing up to and for our leaders.* San Francisco: Berrett-Koehler.

Cheney, G., & Carroll, C. (1997). The person as object in discources in and arouund organizations. Working paper.

Communication Briefings™ (1991, May–June). Traits preferred in employees. *Female Executive,* 12.

Covey, S. R. (1989). *The 7 habits of highly effective people: Powerful lessons in personal change.* New York: Simon & Schuster.

Cummings, L. L., & Anton, R. J. (1990). The logical and appreciative dimensions of accountability. In S. Srivastva, D. L. Cooperrider, & Associates, *Appreciative management and leadership: The power of positive thought and action in organizations* (pp. 257–286). San Francisco: Jossey-Bass.

D'Aprix, R. M. (1976). *In search of a corporate soul.* New York: AMACOM.

Deal, T. E., & Jenkins, W. A. (1994). *Managing the hidden organization: Strategies for empowering your behind-the-scenes employees.* New York: Warner Books.

Denison, D. R. (1990). *Corporate culture and organizational effectiveness.* New York: Wiley.

Drucker, P. F. (1974). *Management: Tasks, responsibilities, practices.* New York: HarperCollins.

Egan, G. (1990). *The skilled helper: A systematic approach to effective helping.* Belmont, CA: Wadsworth.

Farren, C., & Kaye, B. (1996). New skills for new leadership roles. In F. Hesselbein, M. Goldsmith, & R. Beckhard (Eds.), *The Leader of the future* (pp. 175–187). San Francisco: Jossey-Bass.

Felkins, P. K., Chakiris, B. J., & Chakiris, K. N. (1993). *Change management: A model for effective organizational performance.* New York: Quality Resources.

Ford, J. D., & Ford, L. W. (1995). The role of conversations in producing international change in organizations. *Academy of Management Review, 20* (3), 541–570.

French, P. A. (1984). *Collective and corporate responsibility.* New York: Columbia University Press.

French, W., & Bell, C., Jr. (1990). *Organization development* (4th ed.). Englewood Cliffs, NJ: Prentice-Hall.

George, J. M., & Brief, A. P. (1996). Motivational agendas in the workplace: The effects of feelings on focus of attention and work motivation. In B. M. Staw & L. L. Cummings (Eds.), *Research in Organizational Behavior: Vol. 18.* (pp. 75–109). Greenwich, CT: JAI Press.

Gergen, K. J. (1990). Affect and organization in postmodern society. In S. Srivastva, D. Cooperrider, & Associates, *Appreciative management and leadership: The power of positive thought and action in organizations* (pp. 153–174). San Francisco: Jossey-Bass.

Gergen, K. J. (1991). *The saturated self: Dilemmas of identity in contemporary life.* New York: Basic Books.

Gergen, K. J. (1992). Organization theory in the postmodern era. In M. Reed & M. Hughes (Eds.), *Rethinking organization* (pp. 206–226). London: Sage.

Gergen, K. J., & Thatchenkery, T. J. (1996). Organization science as social construction: Postmodern potentials. *Journal of Applied Behavioral Science, 32* (4), 356–377.

Gibb, J. R. (1978). *Trust: A new view of personal and organizational development.* Los Angeles: Guild of Tutors Press.

Hall, D. T. (1996). Protean careers of the 21st century. *Academy of Management Executive, 10*(4), 8–16.

Hall, M. (1996). Increasing leadership capacity to transform organizations. In *The 1996 NLI conference proceeding: Leaders & change* (pp. 129–140). College Park, MD: National Leadership Institute, University of Maryland.

Hammond, S. (1996). *The thin book of appreciative inquiry.* Plano, TX: Kodiak Consulting.

Hammond, S., & Overton, M. (1995). *Lake Miramar's change model.* Plano, TX: Kodiak Consulting.

Handy, C. (1989). *The age of unreason.* Boston: Harvard Business School Press.

House, R. J., & Baetz, M. L. (1990). Leadership: Some empirical generalizations and new research directions. In L. L. Cummings & B. M. Staw (Eds.), *Leadership, partnership and group behavior* (pp. 1–84). Greenwich, CT: JAI Press.

Kasler, D. (1988). Max Weber: An introduction to his life and work. Chicago: University of Chicago Press.

Kelley, R. (1992). *The power of followership.* New York: Bantam Books.

Kouzes, J. M., & Posner, B. Z. (1993). *Credibility: How leaders gain and lose it, why people demand it.* San Francisco: Jossey-Bass.

Kuczmarski, S., & Kuczmarski, T (1995). *Values-based leadership: Rebuilding employee commitment, performance, and productivity.* Englewood Cliffs, NJ: Prentice-Hall.

Kuhn, T. S. (1980). *The structure of scientific revolutions* (2nd ed.). Chicago: University of Chicago Press.

Leavitt, H. (1972). *Managerial psychology* (3rd ed.). Chicago: University of Chicago Press.

Lerner, H. G. (1985). *The dance of anger: A woman's guide to changing the patterns of intimate relationships.* New York: HarperCollins.

Levinson, H. (1968). *The exceptional executive: A psychological conception.* Cambridge, MA: Harvard University Press.

Levinson, H. (1996, July–August). When executives burn out. *Harvard Business Review,* 153–163.

Maccoby, M. (1988). Integrity: A fictional dialogue. In S. Srivastva & Associates, *Executive integrity: The search for high human values in organizational life* (pp. 29–44). San Francisco: Jossey-Bass.

McCall, J. J. (1995). Participation in employment. In W. H. Shaw & V. Barry (Eds.), *Moral issues in business* (6th ed.; pp. 349–357). Belmont, CA: Wadsworth.

McKay, M., Rogers, P., & McKay, J. (1989). *When anger hurts: How to change painful feelings into positive action.* Oakland, CA: New Harbinger.

McLagan, P., & Nel, C. (1996). *The age of participation: New governance for the workplace and the world.* San Francisco: Berrett-Koehler.

McNamee, S., & Gergen, K. (in press). *Relational responsibility*. Thousand Oaks, CA: Sage.

Menken, D. L. (1988). *Faith, hope and the corporation: Sharpening your business philosophy and business ethics.* St. Paul, MN: Phronticterion.

Meyerson, M., (1997, June–July). Everything I thought I knew about leadership is wrong. *Fast Company,*Special Edition: *The New Rules of Business, 1,* 4–11.

Mintzberg, H. (1989). *Mintzberg on management: Inside our strange world of organizations.* New York: Free Press.

Mintzberg, H. (1996, July–August). Musings on management: Ten ideas designed to rile everyone who cares about management. *Harvard Business Review, 73*(4), 61–67.

Nadler, D. A., & Lawler, E. E., III. (1995). Motivations: A diagnostic approach. In B. M. Staw (Ed.), *Psychological dimensions of organizational behavior* (2nd ed.; pp. 27–37). Englewood Cliffs, NJ: Prentice-Hall.

Neilsen, E. H. (1986). Empowerment strategies: Balancing authority and responsibility. In S. Srivastva & Associates, *Executive Power* (pp. 78–110). San Francisco: Jossey-Bass.

Noer, D. M. (1997). *Breaking free: A prescription for personal and organizational change.* San Francisco: Jossey-Bass.

Oliphant, J. (1996, July). *Regarding appreciative inquiry and well-formed outcomes.* Presentation at The Leading Clinic™, Seattle, WA.

Parenti, M. (1978). *The power and the powerless.* New York: St. Martin's Press.

Pfeffer, J. (1981). *Power in organizations.* New York: HarperCollins.

Pinchot, G. (1996). Creating organizations with many leaders. In F. Hesselbein, M. Goldsmith, & R. Beckhard (Eds.), *The leader of the future* (pp. 25–39). San Francisco: Jossey-Bass.

Plamondon, W. N. (1996). Energy and leadership. In F. Hesselbein, M. Goldsmith, & R. Beckhard (Eds.), *The leader of the future* (pp. 265-272). San Francisco: Jossey-Bass.

Reichers, A., Wanous, J., & Austin, J. (1997). Understanding and managing cynicism about organizational change. *Academy of Management Executive, 11*(1), 48–59.

Reichheld, F. F. (1996). *The loyalty effect.* Cambridge, MA: Harvard Business School Press.

Robbins, S. P. (1993). *Organizational behavior: Concepts, controversies, and applications* (6th ed.). Old Tappan, NJ: Simon & Schuster.

Ryan, K. D., & Oestreich, F. K. (1991). *Driving fear out of the workplace.* San Francisco: Jossey-Bass.

Schneider, B., Brief, A. P., & Guzzo, R. A. (1996, Spring). Creating a climate and culture for sustainable organizational change. In *Organizational Dynamics, 24*(4), 7–9.

Senge, P. M., Leiner, A., Roberts, C., Ross, R. B., & Smith, B. J. (1994). *The fifth discipline fieldbook.* New York: Doubleday.

Shull, G. R. (1997, March 11). *400° feedback and feedforward.* Speech presented to Society of Human Resource Managers, Lima, OH.

Smith, D. K. (1996). The following part of leading. In F. Hesselbein, M. Goldsmith, & R. Beckhard (Eds.), *The leader of the future* (pp. 199–207). San Francisco: Jossey-Bass.

Srivastva, S., & Barrett, F. (1990). Appreciative organizing: Implications for executive functioning. In S. Srivastva, D. L. Cooperrider, & Associates, *Appreciative management and leadership: The power of positive thought and action in organizations* (pp. 381–400). San Francisco: Jossey-Bass.

Srivastva, S., & Carten, C. (1996, Winter). Organizational beauty: The art of human relationships. *Academy of Management Organization Development and Change Newsletter,* 8–11.

Srivastva, S., Fry, R. E., & Cooperrider, D. L. (1990). The call for executive appreciation. In *Appreciative management and leadership: The power of positive thought and action in organizations* (pp. 1–33). San Francisco: Jossey-Bass.

Tavris, C. (1989). *Anger: The misunderstood emotion.* New York: Simon & Schuster.

Tetlock, P. E. (1990). Accountability: The neglected social context of judgment and choice. In L. L. Cummings & B. M. Staw (Eds.), *Information and cognition in organizations.* Greenwich, CT: JAI Press.

Trice, H. M., & Beyer, J. M. (1993). *The cultures of work organizations.* Englewood Cliffs, NJ: Prentice-Hall.

Vogt, J. F., & Murrell, K. L. (1990). *Empowerment in organizations: How to spark exceptional performance.* San Francisco: University Associates.

Wanous, J. P., Reichers, A. E., & Austin, J. T. (1994, August). *Organizational cynicism: An initial study.* Presented at the Academy of Management annual meeting, Dallas, TX.

Weick, K. E. (1995). *Sensemaking in organizations.* Thousand Oaks, CA: Sage.

Wheatley, M. (1996, October). Statement made during a presentation in Toledo, OH.

Wheatley, M. J. (1992, October). *Leadership and the new science.* San Francisco: Berrett-Koehler.

Wolfe, D. M. (1988). Is there integrity in the bottom line: Managing obstacles to executive integrity. In S. Srivastva & Associates, *Executive integrity: The search for high human values in organizational life* (pp. 140–196). San Francisco: Jossey-Bass.

Yukl, G. (1990). *Skills for managers and leaders: Text, cases and exercises.* Englewood Cliffs, NJ: Prentice-Hall.

Recommended Reading

Argyris, C. (1990). *Overcoming organizational defenses.* Needham Heights, MA: Allyn & Bacon.

Deal, T. E., & Jenkins, W. A. (1994). *Managing the hidden organization: Strategies for empowering your behind-the-scenes employees.* New York: Warner Books.

Hammond, S. (1996). *The thin book of appreciative inquiry.* Plano, TX: Kodiak Consulting.

Kuczmarski, S. S., & Kuczmarski, T. D (1995). *Values-based leadership: Rebuilding employee commitment, performance, and productivity.* Englewood Cliffs, NJ: Prentice-Hall.

McLagan, P., & Nel, C. (1995). *The age of participation: New governance for the workplace and the world.* San Francisco: Berrett-Koehler.

McNamee, S., & Gergen, K. J. (in press). *Relational responsibility.* Thousand Oaks, CA: Sage.

About the Author

Jane Galloway Seiling is a consultant, writer, and speaker. Founder of Business Performance Group in Lima, Ohio, she is an associate of The Taos Institute in Taos, New Mexico, an organization formed to further the achievement of positive social relationships within families, organizations, communities, and the global arena, and of Kodiak Consulting in Dallas, Texas. She holds a master's degree in organization development.

Seiling's primary professional interest centers around issues inherent in labor-management relationships and how these issues affect the opportunities organizations and their members have to grow and achieve. This interest in membership developed from her personal experience as secretary, assistant to five CEOs, supervisor, customer advocate, and marketing associate. It is Seiling's belief that the success of an organization is dependent on partnerships that go beyond participation, that members at all levels contribute to the success or failure of the organization, and that there are dormant talents and skills within organizations that must be tapped to sustain and/or grow the business and re-enroll members. This requires a new language and a new understanding of the role of the individual member—from the CEO to the professional to the member standing at the machine.

Learn more about the concepts presented in this book by visiting the author's Web site at www.membership.org.

Index